THE DYNAMICS OF OUTPORT FURNITURE

ADAPTATION
AND
CULTURE

WALTER W. PEDDLE

Mercury Series
History Division
Paper 51

Published by
Canadian Museum of Civilization

© Canadian Museum of Civilization 2002

NATIONAL LIBRARY CANADIAN CATALOGUING IN PUBLICATION DATA

Peddle, Walter W.
The dynamics of outport furniture design: adaptation and culture

(Mercury series)
(History Division paper, ISSN 0316-1854; 51)
Includes an abstract in French.
Includes bibliographical references.
ISBN 0-660-18802-3

1. Country furniture — Newfoundland.
2. Painted country furniture — Newfoundland.
3. Furniture — Newfoundland.
4. Furniture, Early Canadian.
I. Canadian Museum of Civilization.
II. Canadian Museum of Civilization. History Division.
III. Series.
IV. Series: Paper (Canadian Museum of Civilization. History Division); no. 51.
V. Title.

NK2442.N5P42 2002   749.211'8   C2002-980109-5

 PRINTED IN CANADA

Published by
Canadian Museum of Civilization
100 Laurier Street
P.O. Box 3100, Station B
Hull, Quebec
J8X 4H2

Publications advisor: Dr. Peter E. Rider
Atlantic Provinces Historian and Curator

Senior production officer: Deborah Brownrigg

Cover design: Phredd Grafix

Front cover photographs:
A c. 1900 pine cross-corner picture frame; Path End, Burin Peninsula, Newfoundland, c. 1900–1910 (National Archives of Canada).

Back cover photographs:
Child's armchair, mid-nineteenth century, south shore of Trinity Bay, Newfoundland; Homemade washstand, Rose Blanche, Newfoundland (Photo: Antonia McGrath); Pine washstand, c. 1900, Lower Island Cove, Newfoundland.

All photographs are courtesy of the author except as noted otherwise.

Canadä

OBJECT OF THE MERCURY SERIES

The Mercury Series is designed to permit rapid dissemination of information pertaining to the disciplines in which the Canadian Museum of Civilization is active. Considered an important reference by the scientific community, the Mercury Series comprises over three hundred specialized publications on Canada's history and prehistory.

Because of its specialized audience, the series consists largely of monographs published in the language of the author.

In the interest of making information available quickly, normal production procedures have been abbreviated. As a result, grammatical and typo-graphical errors may occur. Your indulgence is requested.

Titles in the Mercury Series can be obtained
by calling 1-800-555-5621;
by e-mail to <publications@civilization.ca>;
by Internet to <http://www.cyberboutique.civilization.ca>;
or by writing to:

Mail Order Services
Canadian Museum of Civilization
100 Laurier Street
P.O. Box 3100, Station B
Hull, Quebec J8X 4H2

BUT DE LA COLLECTION MERCURE

La collection Mercure vise à diffuser rapidement le résultat de travaux dans les disciplines qui relèvent des sphères d'activités du Musée canadien des civilisations. Considérée comme un apport important dans la communauté scientifique, la collection Mercure présente plus de trois cents publications spécialisées portant sur l'héritage canadien préhistorique et historique.

Comme la collection s'adresse à un public spécialisé, celle-ci est constituée essentiellement de monogra-phies publiées dans la langue des auteurs.

Pour assurer la prompte distribution des exemplaires imprimés, les étapes de l'édition ont été abrégées. En conséquence, certaines coquilles ou fautes de grammaire peuvent subsister : c'est pourquoi nous réclamons votre indulgence.

Vous pouvez vous procurer les titres parus
dans la collection Mercure par téléphone,
en appelant au 1 800 555-5621,
par courriel, en adressant votre demande à <publications@civilisations.ca>, par Internet, à <http://www.cyberboutique.civilisations.ca>
ou par la poste, en écrivant au :

Service des commandes postales
Musée canadien des civilisations
100, rue Laurier
C.P. 3100, succursale B
Hull (Québec) J8X 4H2

ABSTRACT

Outport furniture is one of the most colourful and distinctive forms of regional furniture in North America, and is a testament to human ingenuity and diversity of expression. The most important attribute of traditional outport furniture, however, may lie in its potential to convey practical messages to the present-day people of Newfoundland and Labrador.

The recent collapse of the North Atlantic cod fishery has created enormous economic and cultural challenges for Newfoundlanders and Labradorians. Although the challenges are great, the people of Newfoundland and Labrador are intrinsically well-equipped to tackle and solve all manner of problems — and not just those arising from the possible demise of the Atlantic fishery. Outport furniture clearly reveals that the forebears of Newfoundlanders and Labradorians were naturally innovative, clever designers, practiced recyclers and masters of adaptation. Because the present-day people of the province continue to have these attributes, this information is a powerful confidence-builder, and could not be more timely.

The items which comprise outport furniture, and country furniture in general, are not simply rural copies of high-style furniture. The initial models on which outport furniture were patterned were items of European country or regional furniture, not high-style furniture. Furthermore, because outport furniture, like the country furniture of other North American and European geographical regions, is a distinctive and legitimate body of furniture in its own right, it can be used as a window into the equally distinctive regional culture of Newfoundland and Labrador. In addition to revealing the character and mindset of the region's people, outport furniture provides important information and insight on how social and economic realities, ergonomics and the physical environment have shaped the local culture.

RÉSUMÉ

L'ameublement des villages de pêche est une des formes les plus pittoresques et les plus distinctives d'ameublement régional en Amérique du Nord. C'est un véritable hommage rendu à l'ingéniosité humaine et à la diversité d'expression. La caractéristique la plus importante de cet ameublement traditionnel, toutefois, réside dans sa capacité de transmettre les messages aux gens qui habitent Terre-Neuve et le Labrador aujourd'hui.

Les habitants de Terre-Neuve et du Labrador se sont trouvés devant d'énormes défis économiques et culturels à la suite du récent effondrement de la pêche à la morue dans l'Atlantique Nord. Bien que ces défis soient de taille, la nature même des gens de Terre-Neuve et du Labrador fait qu'ils sont bien équipés pour s'attaquer à n'importe quels problèmes et à les résoudre – et pas seulement ceux qui proviennent de l'éventuelle disparition de la pêche dans la région de l'Atlantique. L'ameublement des villages de pêche montre clairement que les aïeux des habitants de Terre-Neuve et du Labrador étaient, par nature, des artisans novateurs, d'astucieux concepteurs et des maîtres du recyclage et de l'adaptation. Comme la population actuelle possède toujours ces qualités, cette information agit comme un puissant agent de renforcement de la confiance et ne peut pas mieux tomber.

Les pièces qui constituent l'ameublement des villages de pêche, et l'ameublement rural en général, ne sont pas de simples reproductions paysannes de meubles de grand style. Ce sont des meubles de pays européens et du mobilier régional plutôt que des meubles de grand style qui ont servi de modèle, à l'origine, aux meubles traditionnels des villages de pêche. Par ailleurs, parce que l'ameublement des villages de pêche, comme le mobilier rustique d'autres régions nord-américaines et européennes, constitue un ensemble spécifique et légitime en soi, on peut s'en servir comme une fenêtre qui ouvre sur la culture régionale également spécifique de Terre-Neuve et du Labrador. En plus de révéler le caractère et la façon de penser des gens de la région, l'ameublement des villages de pêche donne d'importantes indications sur la manière dont les réalités économiques et sociales, l'ergonomie et l'environnement physique ont façonné la culture locale.

TABLE OF CONTENTS

FOR RUPERT BATTEN

ACKNOWLEDGMENTS

The material for this book was gathered over a very long period of time with the help of numerous individuals and organizations. It would occupy far too many pages to name them all. But I would be negligent indeed if I did not express a special thanks to my wife, Sally for her encouragement and advice and for accomplishing numerous tedious tasks on my behalf.

The late Rupert Batten and Dr. Gerald L. Pocius encouraged and assisted me from the very beginning of the project. The Newfoundland Museum provided valuable help as well. The Museum's Chief Curator, Penny Houlden, has been particularly supportive, and my colleagues, Frank Barrington and Tim Cohen gave me both physical assistance and moral encouragement. An individual to whom I will be eternally grateful is Ross Bussey who provided me with invaluable information and materials.

Essential scholarly contributions were made by Dr. Bernard D. Cotton, Dr. W. Gordon Handcock, Dr. John Mannion and Matt McNulty. Matt provided me with most of the information concerning Irish vernacular furniture contained in this book.

As well, I am grateful for the important advice, information and/or encouragement given me by Claudia Kinmonth and Dr. Jane L. Cook. And I am especially grateful to Gail Collins for allowing me to use her fine article about her talented grandmother, Elizabeth Gale. I offer thanks also to my son-in-law, Rodney Bussey, for his help with moving items of furniture for photographing.

The following people contributed photographs: Mannie Buchheit, Mike Paterson, Hilary Cook, Gail Collins and Antonia McGrath.

Finally, I would like to thank the former Minister of Fisheries and Aquiculture, Mr. John Efford, for his kind offer of assistance. I was moved by his genuine and passionate interest in the people and the fishing culture of Newfoundland and Labrador.

FOREWORD

I have always been in love with vernacular furniture, the universality of its function, and yet the infinite diversity of its individual expression. It speaks to me of craft, of art, of invention, of quirkiness, of love, of independence, of confidence and much more.

The concept that vernacular furniture could provide an additional and important window to explore regional culture and ethnic origin, as a new research empowerment was first raised seriously by Walter Peddle.

Certainly other comprehensive studies of vernacular furniture from the new world were well aware of national influences from the old world, but none had understood that through applied scholarship these "national influences" could frequently be attributed to very specific regions and areas, which fully supported the more orthodox evidence of migration and emigration.

In most of the old world, travel beyond emigration was limited for the permanent communities who lived in fixed areas through the generations and thereby provided the context for the emergence and perfection of local stylistic preferences. The research of scholars like Dr. Bill Cotton confirms and defines the differentiating features very specifically to local areas.

The study and appreciation of vernacular furniture is in its infancy and deserves and requires more attention and study by scholars, so that it can yield up greater insights and knowledge of the people who created it and communities who use it.

This book on the dynamics of outport furniture is another worthy contribution, which opens the window of understanding significantly wider and gives us a much greater insight to a pioneering and resourceful people, creating a new life and circumstances, but conscious of their roots and sustained and driven by the memories of what they had known.

Outport furniture represents the creation of a new culture from a diversity of sources. It mirrors the endeavors and achievements of its creators. It is a statement of hope, the beginning of permanency in a new place.

Despite the variety of sources for the wood and the simplicity of its joined construction, vernacular furniture often has great presence and is always full of character and quirkiness. Its sometimes misshapen style is always as fit for purpose, as the camel is to the desert.

I recall many years ago acquiring a chair of individual design and coarse construction. It suggested a rather frugal approach to comfort, until I sat in it and found a harmony and balance, which far exceeded modern ergonomic comfort features. The chair is on loan to an institution and I never pass it without sitting down for a pleasant reminder of its virtues.

I know of an executive of a mult-national company in London, who through years of back pain had afforded himself every opportunity of trying new specially designed chair solutions, but to no avail. He was an antique collector of note, and one day when visiting a dealer he saw an oddity — a vernacular joined chair — among the finer stock.

He sat down as a giggle, but he left with the chair, which found a place of honour in his office. He recalled how many high level visitors and fellow back sufferers asked to try it for fun, only to ask, "where can I get one". It may account for the really exceptional price achieved by the chair when it sold at auction, when he passed away a few years ago.

The community who designed, made and used outport furniture experienced the full rigours of life, but their furniture is their practical expression of creating personal home comfort, decoration and usefulness.

Is it too much to believe that it sustained the illusion and comfort of the familiar in a new and different world?

Matt McNulty
Dublin, Ireland
January 2002

INTRODUCTION

Outport furniture is related to that broad category of furniture which is commonly referred to as country furniture. Other names include "vernacular furniture, "painted furniture" and "common furniture". Perhaps the most appropriate name to call it is "regional furniture", since each European and North American region developed its own distinctive brand.[1]

Unlike many people think, country, or regional furniture is not simply a rural (interpret: "inferior") version of high-style furniture. Though its design and decoration has been influenced in varying degrees by its fashionable formal cousin, regional furniture was shaped primarily by factors of regional relevance. For this reason, regional furniture can serve as a window through which regional culture can be effectively explored.

The initial models after which much North American regional furniture was patterned were items of European regional furniture, not high-style furniture. For the most part, European regional furniture had its beginnings towards the end of the seventeenth century when furniture making there branched off in three separate directions[2]:

- the making of elaborately carved items
- the crafting of veneered pieces
- the construction of joined furniture.

Carving and veneering required expensive materials and specialized skill. Consequently, carved and veneered furniture was made mostly for wealthy people who could afford to buy it. Joined furniture, on the other hand, because it was relatively easy to produce and was less costly to make, became the normal product of rural areas.

The technology for crafting joined furniture changed little over the course of the years.[3] Rural furniture remained primarily utilitarian and its design and use were affected less by changing fashions and more by regional realities such as social and economic conditions, available materials, and the type of work people did to make a living. Such factors, needless to say, varied considerably from region to region, and just as each region had its own spoken dialect, foods, music and customs, each also developed its own distinctive brand of furniture.[4]

At the time of early settlement in North America, North American regional differences existed just as they did in Europe. On the island of Newfoundland, for example, unlike elsewhere on the continent, the economy, as well as the culture, was focused almost entirely on the fishery, and the small population was sparsely scattered along almost 1,000 miles of rugged coastline. There were also far fewer native trees in Newfoundland from which to obtain suitable materials for constructing dwellings and making furniture than there were in most other North American regions. White pine, balsam fir, spruce, tamarack and white birch were virtually the only native trees available for this purpose.

When European regional furniture models were introduced to North America, they were not always faithfully reproduced. At least some adaptation was necessary to address differences which existed between their European regional contexts and their new North American ones. Consider, for example, the outport kitchen dresser shown in photo 1. It was patterned after examples made in Dorchester, in the Dorset region of England. Like Dorset dressers (photo 2), it has a free-standing base with cupboards below three drawers, and the panels in the doors and ends are flat. Construction details, including dry mortice and tenon joints which hold the detachable rack in place (photo 3), are also similar. However, unlike Dorset examples, the rack has no back boards. Presumably, they were not needed because the wooden walls of outport houses provided a sufficiently flat surface for resting plates. In Dorset, the walls were usually comprised of stone or 'cob'.

Needless to say, the nature and extent of adjustments which had to be made to any given model varied considerably, depending upon the North American region into which it was being introduced. Furthermore, and this is especially the case for furniture made in the outports of Newfoundland, elements of design from more than one European regional model were sometimes adapted and combined to craft a single item. The kitchen dresser shown in photo 24 is an example. It combines elements of both Irish and English vernacular dresser design, and is discussed in Chapter 1.

In addition to the realities of differing regional conditions and the practice of adapting and combining European regional models, the particular "mix" of models introduced into each North American region was unique, and this too played a major role in the creation of distinctive North American regional furniture.

What constituted a region's mix, for the most part, was determined by the source areas of its early settlers and the ratio of the numbers of settlers coming from them. In Newfoundland, for example, by 1836 settlers numbered 75,000. Almost half were Irish — mostly from the Southeast region — and half were West Country English. Consequently, the majority of European regional furniture models introduced into Newfoundland were from these two British regions. Less significant source areas for Newfoundland and Labrador settlers include other regions of England, Scotland, Wales and the Channel Islands.[5] Needless to say, the ratio of these different groups was by no means spread uniformly throughout the province. A few large bays or sub regions were settled almost exclusively by people from only one of these British regions; others, by various ratios of people from two or more of them.[6] Consequently, though the furniture made throughout the outports of Newfoundland and Labrador share numerous commonalities, distinctive sub-regional characteristics exist.

As time went on, many factors played a role in the evolution of North American regional furniture. Those which contributed to the evolving design of outport furniture include:

- a continuing practice of adapting models in response to evolving conditions, specific needs and a strong creative drive;
- a continuing practice of adapting and combining elements of design from several different models to make one piece of furniture (in later years, even design components of objects other than household furniture were employed);

1.
A painted pine kitchen dresser collected in Trinity East, Trinity Bay, and made circa 1840. Newfoundland Museum collection.

2.
A painted pine dresser with open shelves, made in Dorset, England, circa 1840. Private collection.

3.
Detail of one of the dry mortice and tenon joints.

- an economy and culture which focused almost entirely on the fishery;
- a shortage of suitable furniture making materials, and the practice of recycling;
- a small population which could not support full-time furniture making activities until at least the mid nineteenth century;
- a penchant among outport people generally for working with their hands;
- a relatively unorganized furniture making craft resulting in more freely exercised imagination and invention;
- an occasional use of high style furniture models to craft informal and basically utilitarian pieces;
- a particularly long survival of the outport furniture making tradition and the use of mass-produced furniture as models to make handmade furniture.

Outport furniture is one of the most distinctive bodies of North American regional furniture. Perhaps its greatest value lies in the way it dramatically documents the culture of the remarkable people who made it. Outport furniture clearly reveals that Newfoundlanders and Labradorians admirably managed to eke out a living in a context where they simply had to be resourceful, have great stamina and the courage to persevere in the face of seemingly endless adversity. Most importantly, they succeeded in doing so while retaining a sense of humour and a great capacity for sensitivity and warmth. Awareness of this cultural relevance and significance can bring practical benefits to the present day people of Newfoundland and Labrador.

Relatively few changes occurred in the way Newfoundlanders and Labradorians of European roots lived in the first several hundred years following the days of earliest settlement. However, since the middle years of the twentieth century, the changes to which they have had to adapt have been considerable. The first and most important event which brought them about was the province's confederation with Canada in 1949. At that time, the barter or truck system was abolished virtually overnight in favour of a cash economy. In this particular instance, the changes which followed were, for the most part, of a highly positive nature. The next most significant event, the collapse of the Atlantic cod fishery in 1991, continues to be a disaster, not only for the province of Newfoundland and Labrador, but for numerous Atlantic Canadian fishing communities as well. In Newfoundland and Labrador, however, where the cod fishery has historically shaped almost every aspect of the local peoples' lives, its effects have been particularly devastating. Its collapse has impinged directly, not only the local economy, but also the culture of the entire province.

Though on the distant horizon there is some promise of better days to come through the development of mineral resources and offshore oil reserves, the difficulties the people of Newfoundland and Labrador now face are daunting. These problems, nevertheless, can be overcome. The present day people of Canada's tenth province, like their forebears, are naturally innovative. They are clever designers, practiced recyclers and, perhaps most importantly, masters of adaptation. These talents are in the local gene pool and continue to manifest themselves in today's rapidly changing environment. There is much evidence that Newfoundlanders are at least as well equipped as any contemporary society to tackle and contribute to the solutions of all manner of contemporary problems, including those arising from the possible demise of the Atlantic fishery and even those relating to the world-wide depletion of natural resources and the alarming possibility that the human species is slowly poisoning the planet's delicately balanced eco system. Virtually speaking, there is only one thing preventing Newfoundlanders and Labradorians from exercising the full potential of their capabilities in the twenty-first century: a lack of confidence. It is for this reason, the greatest value outport furniture has, lies in the positive messages it carries for the present day people of the province. The messages are powerful confidence builders, and they couldn't be more timely.

ENDNOTES

1. The concept of regionality, as it relates to vernacular furniture, is discussed in Dr. Bernard D. Cotton's article, "Regional Furniture Studies in the Late Eighteenth and Nineteenth Century Traditions: An Introduction to Research Methods," in *Regional Furniture*, (1987), 1–18.

2. See Edward Lucie-Smith, *Furniture: A Concise History* (London: Thames and Hudson Ltd., 1990), 88–91

3. See Edward Lucie-Smith, *Furniture: A Concise History*, 91.

4. See Cotton's lecture to an invited audience, February 17, 1999, "Noble Furniture — Common Origins", in the *Regional Furniture Society Newsletter, Summer 1999*, no.30, p. 6.

5. See Dr. W. Gordon Handcock's article, "English Settlement in Newfoundland" in *Routes: Exploring the British Origins of Newfoundland Outport Furniture Design*, 28–29 and Dr. John Mannion's article, "The Irish Migration to Newfoundland", also in *Routes*, 30–31.

6. *Ibid.*

CHAPTER 1

THE INTRODUCTION OF BRITISH REGIONAL FURNITURE MODELS TO NEWFOUNDLAND

The large pine sea chest shown in photo 4 is on exhibit at the Fisherman's Museum in Hibb's Cove, Port de Grave, Conception Bay. It could be the oldest surviving piece of outport furniture. It dates to circa 1750 and is made from riven sections of wood. In fact, on close inspection, it is possible to see the concave marks of a 'scrub' plane used to level the irregular marks of the grain caused by splitting the timber. Construction details include lap-jointed corners secured with hand forged nails. This is typical of eighteenth century examples. The strap hinges, which are fitted over the painting, are old replacements for the staple hinges which were originally there. An extremely thin finish of red ochre remains on the surface of the box. The sides and ends are sloped to provide greater stability on the sea.

The original owner of this chest most likely served as a sailor in the British navy. During the seventeenth and eighteenth century, British sailors often traveled to the Near East, and it became a tradition to paint the exotic scenery they encountered, on the underside of the lids of their sea chests. The type of house and potted plants depicted on this particular cover, were commonly seen along the coastline there. This early tradition is unrelated to the nineteenth century one of painting sea-going vessels on the undersides of relatively smaller travelling boxes.

Only a relatively small number of large sea chests have been found in Newfoundland and Labrador, and some of them may not even have been made there. It is quite possible the very earliest examples were made in Britain during the days of the migratory fishery[1], for transporting personal possessions for seasonal voyages to Newfoundland, or for permanently settling there.

4.
A large pine or balsam fir seaman's chest with an illustration painted on the inside of the lid, collected in Sandy Cove, Port de Grave, Conception Bay, circa 1750. Fishermen's Museum, Port de Grave collection.

The vast majority of earliest surviving examples of outport domestic furniture date
to the early nineteenth century, and most were most likely made by British-born settlers,
not by Newfoundland-born residents. In fact, many early pieces closely resemble counterparts made in the settlers' home regions. The outport kitchen dresser shown in photo 5,
for instance, is virtually identical to vernacular examples made in the west of Ireland.
Originally the dresser was built into a kitchen so that one wall served as its back, and the
floor, its bottom. Because the left side was placed against a wall, the left corner at the
top of the base was not made to project as was the one on the right. Such projecting
corners are a distinctly Irish element of design. Another is the integral sides of the base
and the shelf.

Because the left side of this dresser rested against a wall, that side was less accessible
than the right. Consequently the right side got considerably more use. Notice, the wear
on the right projecting corner of the working surface where a knife board would have
been placed for cleaning and sharpening knives, and where a fisherman most likely would
have secured his nets with small nails in order to facilitate mending them (see photo 6).
Such work was often pursued in kitchens during blustery and cold weather when working
in a workshop in an outbuilding would have been uncomfortable and inconvenient. Notice
also the old repair where a piece of wood had split off the front edge. Just as the right
working surface received more use, so too did the right cupboard door. In fact, when
the item was collected, the right door had an old clumsy repair resulting from heavy use,
and it had to be carefully reworked. If you could examine this door closely, you would
see that its framework is assembled differently from that of the left door. However, this
is an original construction detail. Outport furniture, like Irish vernacular furniture, often
displays eccentric characteristics.

The dresser recently has had its numerous layers of paint and dirt removed and its
original grey/green colour simulated. The colour now is virtually identical to the original,
judging by paint specks found in a crevice in one of the wood joints when it was undergoing
restoration. The left side was never painted.

Another example of an outport piece of furniture which closely resembles counterparts
made in the settlers' home regions is the hanging dresser shown in photo 7. It is similar
to ones which were made in Clare, Galway and Tipperary, i.e. the mid-west of Ireland.
In Ireland, hanging dressers normally would be fixed above or to the side of a fireplace
and be used in addition to or instead of a standing dresser. This type of dresser is now
rare in Ireland. In Newfoundland, it is even more rare; only one other relatively large
example has been reported (see photo 96). Both outport examples originally were built
into kitchen walls and were made without backs.

The chair shown in photo 8 is virtually identical to examples made in the West Country
of England. Chairs of this type were perhaps commonly made throughout England during
the seventeenth century. They continued to be made in the northwest and southwest
regions of that country, as well as in New England, Nova Scotia and Newfoundland
until well into the nineteenth century.

5.
An early nineteenth century painted pine kitchen dresser, collected in Tickle Cove, Bonavista Bay. Private collection.

6.
Detail showing wear on the right projecting corner of the working surface.

7.
An early nineteenth century hanging pine kitchen dresser, collected in the North Shore of Conception Bay. Newfoundland Museum collection.

8.
A late eighteenth century turned birch chair with pine seat, of English regional design, collected in Conception Bay. Newfoundland Museum collection.

Photo 9 shows a chair similar to a type made in Ireland. But echoes of its form can be found in Scotland and Wales. The worn scratch and chip carved decoration on the slats (photo 10), however, link this important item specifically to the south of Ireland. The heart motif, as well as a number of other motifs including lozenges, compass stars and flying wheels, were used generally throughout the Celtic areas of Britain as an embellishment. Various chip carved patterns were sometimes employed in combination with them. The incised stars inside the hearts on the slats of this armchair (photo 11), however, is a motif which was used specifically on country furniture made in the southern region of Ireland, especially in the Cork, Limerick and South Tipperary areas. Incised stars are more often found scratched within a wheel. (Additional examples of this regional embellishment can be seen on items shown in photos 115 and 261).

The child's armchair shown in photo 12 displays exceptionally strong Irish characteristics; all of its features occur widely throughout the west of Ireland. Notice that both the crest and intermediate rail are lapped into grooves in the stiles, rather than mortice and tenon jointed. As well, the stretchers between the front and back legs come right through the front legs to support the foot rest (photo 13). The tenons at the top of the front stiles similarly pierce completely through the arm rests. This type of joinery, incidentally, is of a seventeenth century origin. It continued to be used to make Irish country chairs for an additional two hundred years.

The design of the upper part of the chair shown in photo 14 is common to the west coast of Ireland, the Shetland Islands and the Isle of Man. Its design source is probably Irish since the stretcher arrangement is more common there. The chair is made from birch, except for the centre slat, which is oak. The pine seat is not original.

9.
An early nineteenth century birch slat back chair with pine seat, of Irish vernacular flavour, collected in Keels, Bonavista Bay. Private collection.

10.
Detail of the scratch and chip carved decoration.

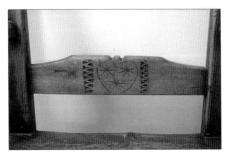

11.
Detail of the incised stars inside one of the hearts.

12.
A mid nineteenth century birch and pine child's armchair having Irish vernacular roots, collected in the south shore of Trinity Bay. The crest rail is an old replacement. Private collection.

13.
Detail of the foot rest.

14.
A nineteenth century slat back chair, collected in Spaniard's Bay, Conception Bay. Private collection.

Photo 15 shows an outport chair which is similar to a general type comprising the most common form of seating during the nineteenth and early twentieth century in rural Ireland. Irish examples, usually have a matted hay or straw rope seat, and are known by the Gaelic term for this material, *sugan.*

The simple but elegant outport chair shown in photo 16 was modelled after an Irish type which some individuals consider to be an example of Irish Shaker furniture. High and low examples were commonly made to accommodate persons who, despite their poor circumstances, enjoyed a bit of comfort. In Ireland it was usual for people to have their own chair in which they felt most comfortable. As a general rule, chairs, which were used at the open fireplace, had low seats, as this example has, to keep the sitters' heads below the smoke line. It is somewhat surprising this particular chair survived many years of usage, considering that the seat frame lacks a front rail. The chair has had its original dark brown finish simulated. Hand forged nails are used in the construction.

Photo 17 shows a chair of Scottish regional inspiration. Its unusually low seat is typical of Scottish chairs which were designed to keep sitters' heads below the smoke which commonly filled the interiors of Scottish sod walled houses. This chair is one of a set of two found in Bay de Verde. A virtually identical third chair was collected in Catalina, Trinity Bay. It is believed all were originally part of the same set. The pine board seat is a replacement. A similar Scottish low chair is shown in photo 18.

At first glance, it might be suspected that the chair shown in photo 19 is the work of a naive maker. In fact, it is an accurate copy of chairs made in both Scotland and Ireland during the mid eighteenth century, which were vernacular interpretations of high-style chairs made by Thomas Chippendale. Furthermore, the chair shown in photo 20 is similar to chairs made in Scotland and Ireland, which were vernacular versions of chairs

15.
A mid nineteenth century birch chair of Irish vernacular persuasion, collected in Upper Island Cove, Conception Bay. Newfoundland Museum collection.

16.
An early nineteenth century birch chair with a low seat of Irish regional inspiration. Collected in Placentia Bay. Private collection.

17.
A painted birch chair of Scottish regional inspiration, collected in Bay de Verde, Conception Bay, circa 1800. Newfoundland Museum collection.

18.
A Scottish low-seat chair circa 1820. Photograph submitted by Dr. Bernard D. Cotton.

19.
A joined birch chair collected in Bryant's Cove, Conception Bay, circa 1840. Newfoundland Museum collection.

20.
A mid nineteenth century birch chair with pine seat, collected in the general area of Harbour Grace, Conception Bay. Newfoundland Museum collection.

designed by Thomas Sheraton. These particular chairs are referred to as Brander Backs. The board seat of the chair shown in the photograph is a replacement, and the original mahogany finish is simulated.

A final example of domestic outport furniture which closely resembles counterparts made in the settlers' home regions is the washstand shown in photo 21. It is virtually identical to examples made in the western coastal area of Ireland.

Most likely, much of the earliest surviving outport furniture closely resembling British regional counterparts, was made by skilled British wood workers who settled permanently in Newfoundland. Beginning as early as 1675, English West Country fish merchants recruited British workers, referred to as "servants", for the Newfoundland seasonal fishery. Their responsibilities mainly involved fishing inshore and curing the catch along the shore-line. Even by the late eighteenth century, when fish merchants had moved offices to Newfoundland and began sponsoring local fishers, the fishery, nevertheless, continued to be migratory in nature. Consequently, British servants continued to be recruited and, by this time, they included skilled wood workers such as joiners, shipwrights, boat builders and carpenters. Many of these tradesmen were employed mainly to build and repair the merchants' Newfoundland residences, fishing premises, schooners and fishing boats. Like migrant workers before them, they usually stayed in Newfoundland for two summers and one winter, but a relatively small number married local women and settled permanently.

While most earliest items of outport furniture closely resemble counterparts made in the various home regions of the settlers, some, like the armchair shown in photo 22, curiously display additional unusual features. Consider the rope twist carving on the stretcher of this chair, for instance. Rope twist carving, is a form of decoration commonly applied to painted furniture made in the southern half of Ireland. Such carving normally was used as a decorative moulding on case furniture. Its use on the front stretcher of this chair is highly unusual. Furthermore, the design of this chair is comprised of a combination of design elements from two or more different Irish regions or sub regions. For example, the shape of the back top rail finds echoes in the presses of County Clare and chairs of the northwest. Another interesting feature is the arms and their shaping. They are a seventeenth century throwback which was retained in the northwest and North Midland areas of Ireland.

Another item displaying curious features is the early nineteenth century birch armchair with pine seat shown in photo 23. According to my knowledgeable Irish colleague, Mr. Matt McNulty, the back uprights are shaped in the manner of western Irish Sugan chairs, which normally have straw seats. On the other hand, the taper at the arm joint on the front legs and the arms are derived from the northeast of Ireland. In Ireland, incidentally, such arms were a throw back to an earlier seventeenth century type which were well worked and finished to enhance comfort. Perhaps the most unique feature of the chair is its back. Similarly shaped and positioned top rails are commonly seen in Irish vernacular examples generally. The other back rails, however, are significantly narrower than their Irish counterparts. The chair presumably was made by an Irish-born and

21.
A mid nineteenth century pine washstand with old paint, collected in Mortier, Placentia Bay. Private collection.

22.
A mid nineteenth century birch armchair, collected in Conception Bay North Shore. Newfoundland Museum collection.

23.
A stylish early nineteenth century birch armchair with pine seat, collected in Catalina Trinity Bay. Private collection.

practiced chair maker, and one can only wonder why he chose to create a unique chair design rather than use an existing familiar traditional model. Adaptation for reason of necessity was most likely not a motive.

The kitchen dresser shown in photo 24 also combines elements of vernacular design from several different areas. In this instance, the distances between them are more widely separated. In the typical manner of Irish design, the rear planks which form the sides or ends of the dresser, are integral with the shelf sides. The shelves, however, are flanked by vertical fluted pilasters, similar to those used in a dresser type made in Dorset, England. Furthermore, the capitals above the pilasters are similar to forms used in some Irish and Cornish furniture. A distinctly Irish element is the front corners of the top of the dresser base which extend outwards. Notice the grooves worn onto the surface of one of them by fishing twine (photo 25). An extended corner of a dresser proved to be a convenient tool over which to hook one end of the fishing mesh.

Another Irish design element is the dresser's relatively shallow depth, a feature often seen in Irish vernacular case furniture. Its purpose was to take advantage of the wall space in one-storey Irish cottages where floor space was at a premium.[2] The cornice and pilasters of the dresser are not the original, but they are accurate replacements. The dresser has been repainted following residues of the original finish. Photo 157 shows the dresser in its "as found" condition.

While some of the earliest items of outport furniture exhibit a combination of vernacular design elements from two or more different British regions or sub regions, others display a combination of British and North American elements. The turned birch armchair shown in photo 26, for example, is patterned generally after English examples. The shape of the spindles, (photo 27) however, were apparently inspired by those commonly found on some North American factory-produced Windsor chairs of the "thumb back" variety (see photos 28 and 29).

24.
An early nineteenth century pine and balsam fir kitchen dresser with integral shelves above, collected in Keels, Bonavista Bay. Newfoundland Museum collection.

25.
Detail of the top right hand corner of the base, which extends outwards.

26.
A turned birch armchair with pine seat,
collected in Catalina, Trinity Bay, circa
1840. Private collection

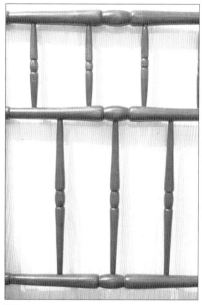

27.
Detail of the spindles.

28.
A "thumb back" Windsor chair, possibly
imported into Newfoundland from Nova
Scotia. Private collection.

29.
Detail of the spindles on the Windsor
chair.

There may have been many factors which contributed to the curious blends of design elements evident in the remarkable furniture discussed above. The most influential one, however, was most likely the basic urge to create. As was suggested in the Foreword, the challenges of pursuing a living in a new way and in a new context must have encouraged experimentation and invention. Irish woodworkers especially would have been so encouraged. In fact, Irish woodworkers already would have been primed to do so.

At about the time the earliest surviving pieces of outport furniture were made, the making of Irish country furniture was in its relative infancy. Irish country furniture is of more recent origin than its counterparts in most regions of Britain where the making of vernacular furniture had been a specialised aspect of the general woodworking skills of peasant craftsmen for centuries).[3] In Ireland it was not until well into the eighteenth century that any equivalent context existed. The state of Ireland had been too turbulent, and a dispossessed and landless peasantry had been too impoverished to give rise to it. Furthermore, the wholesale destruction of native forest and woodlands was also an important factor which precluded the development of an Irish vernacular furniture making tradition until at least the late eighteenth century.[4]

The late eighteenth and early nineteenth century, on the other hand, was a period of significant and relatively peaceful change for rural Ireland. And, in fact, a portion of the peasantry became increasingly affluent. The availability of skilled craftsmen working on the building programmes of the Anglo-Irish gentry, together with an abundant supply of good quality imported pine, resulted in a coincidence of circumstances for the development of a vernacular furniture making tradition. The basis for such a tradition existed in the furnished houses of the English and continental settlers of the sixteenth and seventeenth centuries. These settlers had brought their traditions of furniture construction and use to Ireland. Though none of their furniture has survived, it is most likely this furniture provided the precursors of much of the Irish vernacular furniture with which we are familiar today. Irish furniture historian, Nicholas Loughnan, states: "The subsequent re-interpretation of these vanished early prototypes by eighteenth and nineteenth-century craftsmen working in the decorative tradition of Classical proportion and design, often freely adapted and with varying success, accounts for the peculiarly 'Irish' feel, easier to recognise than define, which characterises so many examples of Irish country furniture."[5]

While a comparatively young vernacular furniture making tradition in Ireland did indeed encourage experimentation and invention, a severe shortage of timber demanded it. By the close of the eighteenth century, timber was in such short supply in Ireland that acts were passed in parliament to penalize anyone who owned wood and could not account for it. Consequently, much of the wood used for furniture making was the cheapest imported softwood.[6] In the absence of wood, furniture makers resorted to a variety of alternatives including straw, willow and even turf. The shortage of wood resulted in a wide range of highly ingenious dual-purpose furniture, which not only saved timber but also required less space and labour.[7]

Yet another factor which likely encouraged innovation was the relatively unorganized nature of the Irish vernacular furniture making craft. Not all furniture makers had formal apprenticeships. Like Newfoundland outport people, a significant number acquired their skills through traditional transmission from their elders.[8]

Often too, Irish furniture makers had to travel over wide distances to find sufficient work. Economic circumstances in many towns were such that local demand was not enough to keep such craftsmen busy on a full time bases. Consequently, many furniture makers were journeymen who would stay in one place only for as long as there was work and then move on to the next town when the need arose.[9] Under the circumstances, it is reasonable to assume that at least some would become familiar with the distinctively designed furniture of several different sub-regions.

Considering all the factors discussed above, it is suspected that the uniquely designed chair shown in photo 23 was made in Newfoundland by a settler who earlier had been a journeyman Irish furniture maker.

In the next two chapters, it will be seen that combining elements of design from more than one model to make an item of furniture was also commonly practiced by the offspring of early British settlers in Newfoundland and Labrador during the nineteenth and early twentieth century. Furthermore, Newfoundland and Labrador born furniture makers faced many of the same kinds of problems Irish vernacular furniture makers faced, and they addressed them in a similar manner.

Endnotes

1. See Dr. W. Gordon Handcock, *So Long as There Comes No Women: Origins of English Settlement in Newfoundland* (St. John's: Breakwater, 1989), for a thorough discussion of the Newfoundland migratory fishery.
2. See Dr. Bernard D. Cotton's article, "Irish Vernacular Furniture", in *Regional Furniture*, The Journal of the Regional Furniture Society, Volume 111, 1989, 1–6.
3. See Nicholas Loughnan, *Irish Country Furniture*, The Irish Heritage Series: 46 (Eason & Son Ltd, Dublin, 1984), 1.
4. *Ibid.*
5. *Ibid.*
6. See Claudia Kinmonth, *Irish Country Furniture, 1700–1950*, (New Haven & London: Yale University Press 1993), 10.
7. *Ibid.*
8. See Kinmonth, *Irish Country Furniture, 1700–1950*, 17.
9. See Kinmonth, 14.

CHAPTER 2

The Products of Shops During the Nineteenth and Early Twentieth Century

Archival records show that British cabinetmakers began setting up shop in St. John's as early as the late eighteenth century. At that time, in addition to England, Scotland, Northern Ireland, Wales and the Channel Islands, Britain also included what is now the Republic of Ireland. One early cabinetmaker, George W. Hancock, who opened a cabinet and upholstery business in St. John's in 1815, advertised in the Newfoundland Royal Gazette of that year that he had had previous experience in his craft in London, Bath, Liverpool, Edinburgh, Dublin and Cork! By the early nineteenth century, there were also British cabinet makers working in Harbour Grace, Conception Bay, Newfoundland's second largest town at the time. Judging by their newspaper advertisements and the relatively few surviving pieces thought to be their products, these craftsmen made highstyle furniture from imported mahogany and other exotic woods. Cabinet makers, however, were few in number and by the second half of the nineteenth century there was only a handful of them practicing in Newfoundland and Labrador. Hutchinson's Newfoundland Directory for 1864, for example, lists seven in St. John's and only one in Harbour Grace.

By about 1860, Newfoundland's first furniture factory, Pope's, was established in St. John's, and by the early twentieth century, a handful of factories were competing in St. John's and in several of the more populated outport communities. In the Census of Newfoundland, 1901, six factories are listed for St. John's with forty eight men employed; one for Avondale with three employed; two for Harbour Grace with six employed; one for Carbonear with eight employed; one for Sandy Point with one employed; one for South Side with one employed; and two for St. George with two employed.[1]

At the same time as cabinetmakers were making fine furniture for prosperous Newfoundlanders in Newfoundland's two largest towns and various grades of both domestic and institutional furniture were being mass-produced in local factories, furniture was being crafted from local timber for fishing families in small outport woodworking shops throughout the island.[2] Presumably, most of the earliest furniture makers who worked in these shops were of British birth. However, migration from Britain virtually ceased by around 1840, and as the nineteenth century progressed, more and more outport furniture was made by the Newfoundland-born descendants of British settlers.

What is known about outport furniture making shops, for the most part, has been gleaned from surviving products and verbal information gathered during field work. Unfortunately, documented information concerning them is virtually limited to several late nineteenth and early twentieth century furniture making enterprises.[3] One thing, however, seems certain: furniture making in the outports, and even wood working in general, could rarely have been pursued as a full time enterprise until the mid or even late nineteenth century. The outport population was too meager and scattered, and simply could not support it. Consequently, furniture making was not an organized craft in the sense it is usually understood. And, furthermore, it appears that, in addition to furniture making, most outport shops performed a wide variety of woodworking tasks including making mouldings, mantel pieces, window and door frames and doors.

The majority of earliest surviving examples of shop-made furniture were modeled after counterparts made in the source regions of the British settlers. The outport kitchen dresser already discussed and shown in photo 1 is one example. At least a dozen virtually identical dressers have been seen in both the north and south shores of Trinity Bay. Other shop-made examples include the items shown in photos 30–32.

It is highly likely that the kitchen dresser shown in photo 30 was made in the same shop as the Dorset type outport dresser shown in photo 1. The bottom edges of the top of the carcase of both dressers are rounded and have a moulding added underneath. Furthermore, both employ dry mortice and tenon joints to hold their racks to the carcase. In this glazed door example, however, two such joints are used on each end, rather than one. In both dressers too, the drawers are similarly lap jointed and forged nails are used in the construction. Both dressers were made with good quality pine and demonstrate a high level of workmanship. In this dresser, however, unlike the dresser with open shelves, dust boards are fitted between the drawers and the cupboard.

The original contrasting colours of the skillfully made chest of drawers shown in photo 31 have been retained. The front and back corners of the drawers, as well as the plinth are fitted together with hand cut dovetail joints, and hand forged nails are used in the construction. There are no dust boards between the drawers.

The original dark red mahogany finish on the chest of drawers shown in photo 32 has been simulated. Significant construction details include the use of dust boards between lap jointed drawers and the use of forged nails. As well, the bottom horizontal rail of each drawer opening is fitted to the ends of the chest using through mortice and tenon joints. Notice that the edges of the top of the chest are chamferred on the bottom side, a detail found on much homemade and shop-produced furniture on the Bonavista Peninsula. This detail is most likely a simplified version of the way in which the bottom edges of the carcase of the outport Dorset-type dresser (photo 1) and the dresser with glazed doors (photo 30) are treated. The wooden pulls with an inset mother-of-pearl button, incidentally, were most likely imported (photo 33).

Some shop-made items continued to be patterned after early British regional models until the late nineteenth century. Amazingly, the design and general appearance of some of this late furniture remained relatively unaffected by the process of adaptation (see photo 34). However, models of British regional origin were not the only ones used by outport shops. There is evidence that, beginning as early as the mid nineteenth century, furniture from Canada and the United States was imported into Newfoundland. Such furniture was most likely also employed as models to make outport pieces. More research, however, needs to be done in this area.

30.
A mid nineteenth century pine dresser with glazed doors, collected in Port Rexton, Trinity Bay. Private collection.

31.
A circa 1850 pine chest of drawers, collected in Belleoram, on the south coast of Newfoundland. Private collection.

32.
A nineteenth century pine chest of drawers, collected in the Bonavista Peninsula. Private collection.

33.
Detail of one of the drawer knobs.

34.
A late nineteenth century pine dresser of British regional design, and similar to the earlier examples shown in photos 1 and 2, collected in the Bonavista Peninsula. Newfoundland Museum collection.

Some shops even patterned their furniture after high style furniture. An example is shown in photo 35. The drawer of this washstand is lap jointed, and forged nails are used in its construction, generally. Another example shown in photo 36 has its original mahogany finish simulated. Forged nails are also used in its construction.

The highly innovative robust parlour sideboard shown in photo 37 is most likely one-of-a-kind. It is generally of Regency flavour, but is endowed with embellishments powerfully symbolic of fertility. It was most likely made as a special wedding gift.

It appears for example, that the backboard of this sideboard is shaped to suggest the upper portion of a coniferous tree, yet is curiously crowned with a shape resembling a deciduous tree leaf (photo 38). The pine pilasters forming the corners of the front of the carcase are three-quarter turned. Those applied to the rear of the sides are quarter turned; and those applied horizontally to the front of the carcase and on the ends, are half turned. The worn gold finish on the applied roundels (one is missing) on the backboard is the original. However, the finish on the remainder of the sideboard is a simulation of the original. It consists of a dark brown paint contrasting with naturally finished panels, applied lozenges and turnings. Other construction details include the lap jointed corners of the drawers and the use of forged nails. As well, there is a dust board fitted between the two half width drawers and the cupboard.

35.
A mid nineteenth century washstand retaining its original paint under several old overcoats, collected in King's Cove, Bonavista Bay. Private collection.

36.
A pine and birch tilt-top pedestal table of Regency inspiration, collected in Harbour Grace, Conception Bay, mid nineteenth century. Private collection.

37.
An imaginatively designed nineteenth century pine sideboard collected near Long Island in Notre Dame Bay. Private collection.

38.
Detail of the crowning shape at the top of the backboard.

By the end of the nineteenth century, British and North American factory forms became the chief source of models. Nevertheless, it is interesting that the construction and appearance of some relatively late items of shop-made outport furniture are strikingly similar to examples of British vernacular furniture made during the mid and late nineteenth century, suggesting that some aspects of furniture making in Britain and the outports continued along very similar paths long after migration to Newfoundland had ceased. For example, the general appearance, the type of wood used, construction details of the case, and the finish of the late nineteenth century outport cupboard shown in photo 39 are similar to the earlier cupboard shown in photo 40, which was made in Cornwall, England. The outport cupboard is partly made from reclaimed timber; the upper and lower doors are paneled, and the drawer is assembled using butted and nailed joints. The sides of its English counterpart are paneled, and their front edges are round moulded in a similar manner to Cornish case furniture. Interestingly, the English cupboard, like the Newfoundland example, may have been made partly from reclaimed material. The framework of the glazed door, for example, is thicker than that of the carcase, suggesting the door initially may have been constructed for an entirely different item.

The most significant feature linking the two cupboards is the close similarity in cornice construction, which is rooted firmly in West Country tradition. The cornices of both examples are made with a simple shaped moulding surmounted with a flat section nailed to the top, and thin strips nailed to the carcase underneath — a method used in West Country case furniture construction.

Another example of late shop-made outport furniture which is similar to examples of relatively late British vernacular furniture is the pedestal table shown in photo 41 beside its English relative. The type of flat sawn legs supporting the two tables are of a type commonly used on nineteenth century English West Country examples. Such legs are a feature which persisted from the seventeenth century. The two tables are shown as they were displayed in the Newfoundland Museum's Travelling exhibit, *Routes: Exploring the British origins of Newfoundland Outport Furniture Design*.

Much of the most distinctive furniture produced by outport furniture making shops was that which combined elements of furniture design from more than one model. The large decorated backboard of the handmade outport sideboard shown in photo 42, for instance, is of popular late nineteenth century Art Nouveau persuasion, while its relatively chaste rectilinear carcase, except for the slightly curved feet, was patterned after local vernacular kitchen dresser bases (examine, for example, the drawer and door arrangement and the narrow central panels on the dresser base shown in photo 24). The backboard of this sideboard (photo 43) is of special interest. The applied hand carved fiddlehead motif, the border of sprig-leaf incising outlining the backboard, and the sprig-leaf incising on the front edges of the shelf, were made using simple hand tools. The spindles supporting the shelf are hand carved, not lathe turned. Curiously, the carcase was given a slightly different primer coat than was the backboard. The now "crackled" finish on the carcase reveals a white painted undercoat, while the backboard has no such undercoat. There

39.
A late nineteenth century pine kitchen cupboard collected in Keels, Bonavista Bay. Newfoundland Museum collection.

40.
A circa 1850 pine food and general storage cupboard made in Cornwall, England. Private collection.

41.
Left : A pedestal table made in Cornwall, England, circa 1840. Private collection. Right: A late nineteenth century pine and birch pedestal table possibly collected in Cupid's, Conception Bay. Newfoundland Museum collection.

42.
A late nineteenth century pine dining room sideboard collected in King's Cove, Bonavista Bay. Private collection.

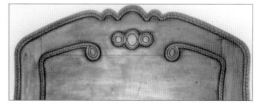

43.
Detail of the backboard.

could be several reasons for this discrepancy. Some could simply be related to the fact that recycled timber was used in the construction. In any case, careful examination of the base and the backboard has indicated they were not "married". The drawers are lap-jointed, and round wire nails are used.

The pedestal table shown in photo 44 is another example of complex design. It curiously has two drop leaves and its pedestal combines features of pedestals of both early tilt-top tripod tables and those of the late Victorian era, which usually had four legs. Notice that the turned pendent at the bottom end of the pedestal is shaped like a turnip. Such a shape was more commonly employed as a foot on tables, chairs and case pieces, and is referred to as a "turnip foot".

The chair shown in photo 45 appears to be partly modeled after a washstand or some other similar item. It was not made to be a potty. It was most likely designed, to address some individual's special needs. For example, the "splashboards" attached to the seat may have been put there to help prevent an elderly or infirm person from accidentally spilling onto the floor. The fact that the seat is unusually low supports this possibility. The chair is painted green and the crest rail, highlighted in gold. The painted pine washstand beside it, incidentally, was collected in King's Cove, Bonavista Bay and dates to the mid nineteenth century.

Perhaps, the shop-produced items which most reflect aspects of the history and evolution of the local culture are those which combine features of early Irish vernacular furniture with late factory forms. For example, the general shape of the both the dresser and its matching washstand shown in photos 46 and 49, including the arrangement of drawers and doors, is similar to that of sets which were mass-produced in British and North American factories during the late nineteenth century. However, decorations on the dresser, including the lozenges and the fretted motifs on the frieze (photos 47 and 48),

44.

A late nineteenth century pine and birch tripod table collected in Keels, Bonavista Bay. Private collection.

45.

An early twentieth century chair reputed to have been made by Mr. Fred Tucker, a Port de Grave woodworker and furniture maker. Private collection.

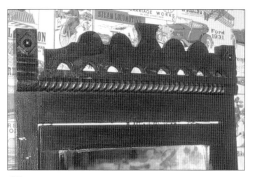

47.
Detail of the frieze.

46.
A late nineteenth century pine bedroom dresser collected in the North Shore area of Conception Bay. Private collection.

48.
Detail showing the top of the projecting stile at one end of the dresser. The ball within a diamond is carved in relief.

49.
The matching washstand to the dresser shown in photo 46. Private collection.

can be traced to a much earlier time and to Southern Ireland. Interestingly, according to the author's Irish colleague, Matt McNulty, the frieze combines these southern Irish motifs in an untypical way.

The inspiration for the carved rope twist mouldings on both the dresser and the washstand can also be traced to Southern Ireland. Such carving is a nautical reference and was commonly used to by cabinet makers throughout Britain to decorate high-style furniture. It began to be used extensively in the early nineteenth century following its growing popularity arising from Nelson's naval battles. However, in Southern Ireland, carpenters commonly used rope twist carving to embellish painted or country furniture. Notice that rope twist carving is employed on the towel rail of the washstand (photo 50). Like the similar carving enhancing the stretcher of the outport chair discussed earlier, this is a highly unusual context in which to find it. Normally such carving was employed as a moulding around the edges of frames and panels.

The most unusual detail of the washstand discussed above is hidden behind its apron (photo 51). While on casual inspection the washstand seems to sit directly on the floor, in actual fact, it is supported on four small peg-like feet. The matching dresser also originally stood on similar feet. However, they have long since been removed, presumably because they became damaged. This type of foot was used on items of early Irish furniture to address the problem of having to stand on damp earthen floors. They were practical because they were easily replaced when they rotted or received excessive wear and tear. Such feet began to appear on some Irish furniture from 1730 onwards. They are closely related to the "soles" applied to the feet of drop leaf tables and the duck feet on Irish Dressers. It would seem that this type of foot had no practical purpose on this washstand and its matching dresser, however. Nineteenth century outport bedrooms, which mostly were located on the second level, had wooden, not clay, floors. Evidently, tradition can be exceedingly tenacious!

Other case pieces having "disposable" peg feet have been found in the same general area as the bedroom set discussed above. The washstand shown in photo 52, for example, combines the general form and drawer and cupboard arrangement of popular factory examples of its day with such feet and with a myriad of additional design elements. Presumably this washstand was made in the same shop as was the example shown in photo 49. But, it was most likely a one-of-a-kind creation, perhaps a commissioned piece or a love token. After its photo was taken, its current owner was able to uncover a painted eye on each of the swans' heads. A somewhat similar homemade version of this washstand, collected from the same general area, is shown in photo 105.

Locally growing timber such as pine, white birch, balsam fir, tamarack, and spruce, were the woods most commonly employed for outport furniture making. By the late nineteenth century, however, with the increase in mass production and the resulting shipping by rail and coastal vessels, used packing crates and other wooden containers became plentifully available. The boards, which were already cut, seasoned and free for the taking, were saved and used to make furniture. Attesting to this practice are the

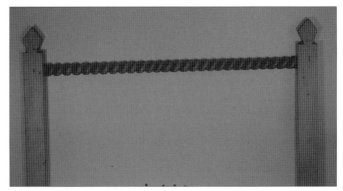

50.
Towel rail of washstand.

51.
Peg feet of washstand.

52.
An elaborately decorated late nineteenth century pine washstand having "disposable" feet and a harp, shaped to suggest the heads and necks of two swans facing in opposite directions, collected in the Conception Bay, North Shore area. Private collection.

stencils and labels of both local and foreign merchants which can be commonly found on the interiors and other hidden surfaces of late outport furniture. The washstand shown in photos 53 and 54 indicates that Britain contributed more than design and decoration to the making of outport furniture.

In addition to packing case material, boards from demolished buildings and other structures were also saved and recycled for furniture making (See photos 290 and 291).

The high incidence of recycling materials to make furniture, and the exceedingly poor quality of some materials that were used suggests there was a serious shortage of good quality, locally growing timber in Newfoundland during the late nineteenth and early twentieth century. But, if this was indeed the case, it was not the only reason recycling was popular. Consider, for example, the bedroom chest of drawers (photo 55) which was made by Albert Rodgers[4], a late nineteenth and early twentieth century Harbour Grace furniture maker. The chest was made from a large shipping crate and is almost certainly a one-of-a-kind example of his work. Pine boards were nailed over the rough wood of a hemlock shipping crate to provide a smoothly finished top and ends for the chest (photo 56). The framework to hold the drawers was built into the open side of the box and the drawers were dovetail jointed. Interestingly, only the left end was embellished with a reeded lozenge. Presumably, the chest was made for a specific corner of a bedroom where the other end would not be seen. The item was originally painted red. Its present grained finish and the lozenge which is painted on the right end were applied at a later date, perhaps when the chest was moved to a new location.

Mr. Rodgers used this piece in his own bedroom, and there is no evidence whatsoever to suggest he imposed such innovative creations on his customers. The furniture he sold employed only insignificant amounts of recycled timber — if any — and was designed using wooden templates (see photo 124). The making of Rodgers' chest of drawers from a shipping box was most likely inspired by an unbridled creative impulse, a good-natured sense of humour and an attitude shared by virtually all outport people: nothing was to be discarded which had potential to be put to some new use.

Several late outport furniture making enterprises were more like factories than like shops. Though they used only hand tools and simple machines powered by hand or foot, these shops resorted to strategies of mass production. Perhaps the most thoroughly documented example of such is that of Henry William Winter of Clarke's Beach, Conception Bay.[5]

During the late nineteenth and early twentieth century, Mr. Winter (photo 57) mass-produced furniture using simple hand tools and a few primitive machines. During the early years of his business, he experimented using wind power (photo 58). For the most part, however, the devices he employed included a foot-powered jig saw, a foot-operated lathe and a large lathe which could either be driven manually or powered by a dog.

According to family sources, Winter received no special training as a furniture maker. Before he pursued furniture making as a full-time venture, he had been trained by a relative, Tom Smart, as a wheelwright.

54.
Detail of the back and underside of the washstand.

53.
A late nineteenth century refinished washstand made of assorted woods, including shipping crate material, collected in Shearstown, Conception Bay. Private collection.

55.
A chest of drawers made by Albert Rodgers in Harbour Grace, Conception Bay, from a discarded shipping crate, circa 1900. Newfoundland Museum collection.

56.
A rear view of the chest of drawers showing the metal strap still attached to the shipping box from which it was made.

In addition to making domestic furniture, Winter made sulkies (small two-wheeled horse drawn carriages) and sleighs, as well as the necessary harnesses for them. He painted and repaired carriages, made picture frames, made church furniture including pulpits, made caskets and, using his hearse, performed some of the services of an undertaker.

The domestic items Winter made were mostly parlour and bedroom pieces (see photos 59–62). He used mainly pine, birch and recycled timber obtained from packing cases for this purpose. During the summer months, he made and stock piled the parts and during the fall he assembled them.

Winter's pieces, particularly his parlour sideboards, are very distinctive. Though he made several different versions of sideboards, all have many features in common. The example shown in photo 59 is most likely one of his early versions.

This particular sideboard has a crowning gallery over a long shelf enclosed by spindles (Winter's later examples, like the one shown in photo 60, usually have a large mirror centred in the backboard). The shelf or platform on the back of the top of the base which resembles a step rising to the backboard, is an especially distinctive feature of all his sideboards. Another is the rounded heavy board applied to the drawer front. As well, the applied panels with scooped corners flanking the cupboard doors are a common feature of many of his sideboards. On some of his earliest examples, however, heavy, half-turned balusters are applied there instead.

The sideboard doors of this example are comprised of planks having simulated panels. As well, embellishments include applied split spindles and rosettes similar to those seen

57.
Henry William Winter posing for his photograph, early twentieth century. Exact date and photographic studio is unknown.

58.
A photograph showing the road in front of Winter's furniture making shop in Clarke's Beach, during the early years of his business when he experimented with wind power.

59.
A typical parlour sideboard made mostly of pine by Henry William Winter of Clarke's Beach, Conception Bay, early twentieth century. Note that the stamped metal back plates of the drawer pulls are missing. Newfoundland Museum collection.

60.
A Winter sideboard employing shamrocks as a decorative motif. Private collection. This particular version is only one of several which have a mirror centred in the backboard.

61.
Detail of the shamrocks painted on the drawer front.

62.
A pine and birch parlour couch made by Henry William Winter, retaining its original dark red finish, yellow line decoration and upholstery. Newfoundland Museum collection.

flanking the drawer. These are all commonly found on Winter's pieces. Like much of Winter's parlour furniture too, the sideboard is finished with varnish or shellac over a dark stain. The typical contrasting line drawing and painted motifs, such as bell flowers and sprig leaves, were done free hand in yellow paint. Typical construction details include mortice and tenon joints in the framing of the front of the carcase, as well as on the framing of the real panels on the end frames. Round nails and lap and butt joints for joining the corners of drawers are also typical.

It is tempting to suspect a link between Winter's furniture and vernacular furniture of southern Ireland. Winter, after all, was exceptionally fond of using fan, or shell carvings (see photos 63 and 65), and this motif was commonly used in the coastal communities of southern Ireland to embellish painted furniture. This suspicion is heightened by the hand painted shamrock motif on the drawer front of the sideboard shown in photo 61.

Perhaps the most popular items Mr. Winter produced are his parlour couches. Decorations on the typical example shown in photo 62 includes applied roundels, half round or "D" shaped disks and sunburst or fan carvings (photo 63), all of which are highlighted with yellow line drawing. Other decoration includes late nineteenth century factory-inspired sprig leaf incising (photo 64) and a crowning feature on the backboard which includes two small carvings of dog's heads facing in opposite directions. This most unusual motif was a tribute to the family dog who, for many years, powered Winter's large lathe. Not all Winter's couches display this particular motif.

The upholstery of this couch is typically painted sail cloth or cotton duck; the stuffing, sea grass gathered from a nearby river. One informant recalls that, around 1929, Mr. Winter would pay five cents a bag for this material, which was also referred to as "eel grass". Winter's parlour couches, like other shop-made examples, were sprung. Also like numerous other shop-made couches of his day, the number of springs employed were far too few in number.

Perhaps Winter's most impressive creation is the large decorated sideboard he was commissioned to build for the Roman Catholic rectory in Brigus. It is shown in photo 65. This imposing item with its many open and enclosed galleries is profusely embellished with his typical furniture decorations. They include fan carvings, roundels, door casing rosettes, turned spindles, split spindles and balusters. The fan or sunburst on each drawer front (photo 66) was carved in relief using a simple hand tool. The spindles and roundels (photo 67) were shaped on Winter's treadle operated lathe, while the heavy split balusters fixed to the base were thrown on his dog-powered device. Significant construction details include the simulated panelling on the ends of the base and the doors. The original dark stain and finish has been simulated.

Judging by the large amount of Mr. Winter's furniture which has been recorded in homes in a wide area around Clarke's Beach, he competed successfully with other local furniture making enterprises and mail order catalogues of the day. Also attesting to the popularity of his products are the many shop-made and homemade pieces which were

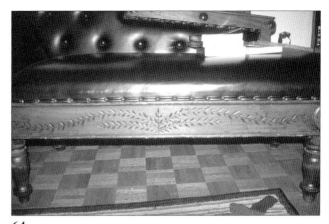

63.
Detail of sunburst and "D" shaped applied carvings on a Winter couch.

64.
Detail showing the sprig leaf incising on the apron of a Winter couch.

66.
Detail of the fan carving on the front of one of the drawers.

65.
A robust pine and spruce sideboard built by Henry William Winter for the Roman Catholic rectory in Brigus, Conception Bay, circa 1900. Newfoundland Museum collection.

67.
Detail of the crowning gallery enclosed by spindles.

modeled after or inspired by his furniture. Although a relatively tiny sample, these items suggest the almost infinite variety of innovative designs which can be potentially achieved through the process of adaptation.

A typical Winter feature on the sideboard shown in photo 68, for instance, is the stepped gallery underneath the mirror. In this example, however, the gallery is enclosed with spindles and the shapes of the spindles and the applied roundels are not of Winter's style. Instead, they take their inspiration from late nineteenth century mass-produced furniture.

While the homemade sideboard shown in photo 69 generally resembles Winter's parlour examples, its construction, in many respects, is actually more sophisticated than Winter's normal work. The panels in the ends and the doors, for example are real ones, left free in their mortice and tenoned frames, to expand and contract as changes in relative humidity dictate. The sideboard's maker, Mr. William Richards, initially worked as a fisherman, but eventually built and operated a general store in Bareneed. According to senior members of his family, he did not make furniture for commercial purposes. Consequently, he was not compelled to "mass produce" or take short cuts with the relatively few pieces he did make to compete with rivals. Instead, he enjoyed the luxury of having sufficient time to employ appropriate joinery techniques.

Details inspired by Henry William Winter are not always immediately obvious. Examine, for example, the sideboard shown in photo 70. At first glance, there seems to be precious little about it that might be connected to Winter. On close inspection, however, it will be seen that there is, in fact, a stepped open shelf or gallery at the back of the base, a distinctive Winter feature. But it is, significantly smaller than Winter's version. Furthermore, this box-like structure, which on Winter's examples encloses wasted space, has been adapted to hold a small drawer. Curiously, the drawer has no hand grasp or pull, making it necessary to remove the sideboard's entire backboard from the base in order to gain access to it. Perhaps the most innovative example of an adapted Winter design element are the split bells which are applied along with other split turnings on the front of the sideboard (photo 71). On Winter's sideboards, small bellflowers are commonly painted in a line format (see photo 59). The sideboard, incidentally, retains its original brown stain and clear finish. The highlighting of the applied ornamentation with gold or bronze paint, however, may be a more recent enhancement. See photo 45 for an unusual chair which retains its original painted finish including a gold-painted crest rail. It was collected from the same source and was most likely made by the same maker.

While Winter's influence is not easy to recognize on some pieces, on others it is very apparent. The couch shown in photo 72, for example, deviates little from its Winter model. Compare it with the Winter couch shown in photo 62. For the most part, the differences which can be found between the two couches are a result of the maker's relative inexperience and the fact he had fewer tools with which to work.

68.
An early twentieth century parlour sideboard collected in North River, Conception Bay, and inspired by parlour examples made by Henry William Winter. Newfoundland Museum collection.

69.
An early twentieth century sideboard patterned after parlour examples made by Winter. Private collection. The sideboard was photographed in a boarded-up house in Bareneed, Conception Bay, around 1999.

70.
An early twentieth century parlour or dining room sideboard of assorted woods, possibly made by Fred Tucker (locally referred to as "Joiner Fred"), a Port de Grave, Conception Bay wood worker and furniture maker. Private collection.

71.
Detail showing four of the applied bells, along with other split and applied decorations.

Another example of an item which has easily recognizable details inspired by
Mr. Winter is the highly decorated washstand shown in photo 73. It is most likely the
result of a joint effort between a Port de Grave furniture maker, Fred Tucker, and a local
resident, John Mugford. While Tucker possibly made the washstand, Mugford, presumably
carved it before it was assembled, to give to his future wife or a close family member, as
a wedding gift. Several informants are of the opinion that Mr. Mugford did not make
large items of furniture, but made picture frames which he enjoyed embellishing with
carving (see photo 279).

 Several very similar washstands, but without the carved decoration (see photo 74),
have been seen in the community of Port de Grave. It is suspected they were a standard
product of Tucker's shop. All had the two-layered aprons, the edges of which were most
likely inspired by those seen on late eighteenth century high-style tables (photo 75).
The addition of the incised carving and drilled decoration on the apron of this particular
washstand, gives the impression of delicate lace.

Perhaps the most impressive carvings on the washstand are the two fan or sunburst
motifs on the backboard (photo 76). Fan carvings were commonly used by Irish carpenters
to decorate furniture made in Southern Ireland. Photo 77, for instance, shows an Irish
settle bed which has been stripped of its painted finish. The corners of its panels are
decorated with shell or fan shell carvings. It was photographed at Johnstown Castle,
near Wexford. The source of their inspiration in the case of the outport washstand,
however, was almost certainly much closer to home. Incidently, notice that the carved
pattern creating a border around the outside edges of the fan carvings on the washstand
are similar to the chip carved patterns on the front of the hanging wall box shown in
photo 188.

Fan carvings in various versions were commonly employed by Henry William Winter
(see photos 62 and 65), whose shop was located in nearby Clarke's Beach. Winter was
also fond of using sprig leaf incised designs in combination with fan carvings (photo 62).
These two embellishments were used on this washstand, but the sprig leaf pattern has
been cleverly adapted to more appropriately reflect the occasion for which the washstand
was to be given. Instead of leaves, round depressions are drilled to suggest seeds. The

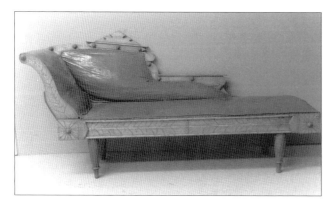

72.
*An early nineteenth century
homemade parlour couch modeled
after examples of Henry William
Winter, collected in Clarke's Beach.
Newfoundland Museum collection.*

73.
An early twentieth century washstand having carved motifs and other decoration inspired by those employed by Henry William Winter. Private collection.

74.
A similar painted washstand to the example shown in photo 73, and photographed in Port de Grave during the 1970s. Private collection.

75.
A late eighteenth century mahogany table on display at the Commissariat House, St. John's.

76.
Detail of sunburst or fan carvings in photo 73.

77.
A Mid nineteenth century Irish vernacular settle bed photographed in Johnstown Castle near Wexford in Ireland, but collected in east county Waterford.

seeds, of course, symbolically express the hope and expectation of a fertile union. The fact they are also used apart from the sprigs to enhance borders, to outline other motifs and to fill in empty spaces, underscores the importance of this hope and expectation.

Other decorations on the washstand include incised hearts having three identical circular designs carved inside their borders (photo 78). Compare this design with the similar scratch-carved motif on the back of the chair shown in photo 9. Perhaps what we have here is a carved version of the star motif which was often incised on vernacular furniture made in South East Ireland.

Apart from Mugford's embellishments, the washstand also displays other evidence of Winter's inspiration, most particularly in the use of applied roundels on the front of the towel rail supports and the applied baluster on the backboard. Roundels were frequently applied on Winter's parlour furniture, while applied balusters normally crowned his bedroom dressers and early versions of his washstands.

The washstand was made partly from recycled pine boards; birch was used for the turned legs; and oak was used to make the front towel rail supports. The original oak grained finish has been simulated.

Few people would think that the inspiration for the mantle shown in photo 79 could be traced to Winter. Nevertheless, the author suspects that narrow beaded boards which were arranged around the arch in a novel way, were done so to suggest a sunburst or fan design, a motif frequently employed by Henry William Winter. Though these boards resemble a mass-produced type commonly used locally for ceilings and wainscoting, they are, in fact, hand shaped. The five pointed stars at the base were incised and enhanced with paint. The current finish on the mantle, however, is not the original. The mantle had been left outdoors, exposed to the ravages of the harsh Newfoundland climate. Consequently, virtually none of its protective paint survived.

The furniture making tradition in the outports virtually died soon after Newfoundland became Canada's tenth province in 1949. However, in recent years, several commercial furniture making enterprises have been launched in the outports. One such business is Paterson Woodworking, located in Upper Amherst Cove, Bonavista Bay.[6]

Paterson Woodworking makes furniture based on earlier outport models, from local woods. The models, however, are adapted to address contemporary realities and needs. The company's founder, Mr. Mike Paterson (photo 80), commented in a recent interview: "Relatively few pieces of older outport furniture are available for purchase, and what is available was not designed with contemporary living in mind."

An example of the products Paterson Woodworking makes is the kitchen dresser shown in photo 81. It was modeled after the early nineteenth century pine dresser shown in photo 24. The model, which has already been discussed, is an unusual mixture of Irish and English regional furniture design. It has no back because it had been built as an integral part of a kitchen. Paterson Woodworking made their version of this dresser free standing by adding a back to it. Furthermore, their dresser was made deeper than the model, which, like much Irish case furniture, was unusually shallow. However, most of the

78.
Detail of circle motifs inside an incised heart in photo 73.

79.
An early twentieth century mantlepiece, collected in Coley's Point, Conception Bay. Private collection.

80.
A January 2002 photograph of Mr. Mike Patterson in his workshop in Upper Amherst Cove.

81.
A contemporary pine dresser made by Paterson Woodworking, and modeled after the early outport kitchen example shown in photo 24.

details, which in the original item had resulted in an aesthetically pleasing new design based in Newfoundland culture, were retained. These details include: the ends of the base and the shelves which are integral in the manner of Irish dressers; the outwardly extending corners at the top of the base, which are another distinctly Irish element; the vertical fluted pilasters which are similar to those employed on dressers made in Dorset, England; and the capitals above the pilasters, which are similar to those used on both Cornish and Irish dressers.

Paterson and his co-workers sometimes deviated even more boldly from the design of their traditional outport models. In the free-wheeling style of many earlier outport furniture makers, they combined design elements which normally wouldn't be brought together, to make their products more visually attractive. For example, they make knife sharpening boxes (normally unadorned utilitarian items) enhanced with chip carving, and turned chairs of traditional design, decorated with brightly painted designs of contemporary flavour.

Because traditional outport models and adaptation play a major role in the design of their products, Paterson woodworking is giving new life to many of the aspects of traditional outport design which document the evolution of the outport fishing culture from its British roots.

Endnotes

1. Information concerning Newfoundland's early cabinet makers and factories was outlined in Walter W. Peddle, *The Forgotten Craftsmen* (St. John's: Harry Cuff Ltd., 1984).

2. See Walter W. Peddle, *The Traditional Furniture of Outport Newfoundland* (St. John's: Harry Cuff Ltd., 1983), for a discussion and photographic inventory of outport furniture.

3. See Peddle, *The Forgotten Craftsmen*.

4. See Peddle, *The Forgotten Craftsmen*, 51–60.

5. See Peddle, *The Forgotten Craftsmen*, 61–76.

6. See Peddle's article, "Survival And Revival: Fruits of an Historical Union", in *Wood: The Beauty of Objects* (Robinson-Blackmore Printing and Publishing, St. John's, 1999), 7–11, for a brief discussion of Mike Patterson.

CHAPTER 3

THE FURNITURE OF HANDY OUTPORT PEOPLE DURING THE NINETEENTH AND EARLY TWENTIETH CENTURY

From the time of earliest settlement in the seventeenth century until at least the mid nineteenth century, it appears almost certain the sparse outport population could not support the full-time activity of professional tradesmen. Furniture making, along with numerous other necessary tasks, were accomplished by handy fishers, as time could be found, between fishing seasons. Furniture making skills were acquired in the same manner as those required to build boats and to perform a range of other relatively complicated work including coopering, black smithing and general carpentry work: through traditional transmission from the older members of family and community to the younger. It was essential that outport people acquire varying degrees of such skills. Each individual simply had to be self-reliant to a very large degree merely to eke out a subsistence living. Furthermore, in addition to being self reliant, it was also necessary for fishers to find employment between fishing seasons as a sailor or a logger, or doing some or all of the work of one or more of a variety of specialized tradesmen, if such work could, in fact, be found. Even formally trained and practiced tradesmen such as shipwrights, joiners, blacksmiths and coopers fished and did work which, in more normal circumstances, would have been the responsibility of other kinds of specialists. But fishing was the driving force behind all this activity, and everything revolved around it. Considering these facts, it is not at all surprising that a relatively large amount of outport furniture continued to be home-made by handy outport people until well into the twentieth century, a time when mass produced furniture was plentifully available elsewhere in Europe and North America, and was relatively inexpensive to buy. Furniture making simply became a traditional activity that numerous outport people put their hands to regardless of the level of their practiced skills or their inherent abilities. There is even an example of a remarkable twentieth century outport woman, Elizabeth Gale, who pursued furniture making. Her accomplishments in this regard are particularly impressive considering that outport women already shouldered more than their fair share of the burden of essential work. They rarely had time to think about, let alone make, household furniture.

It is often difficult to distinguish between the homemade products of handy outport fishers and that of outport woodworking shops. Both used similar materials and tools, employed similar models and made equally innovative furniture. Furthermore, handy outport people often possessed a similar degree of furniture construction knowledge and a similarly wide range of woodworking skills as practiced outport furniture makers had.

Like practiced outport furniture makers, handy outport people used locally growing timber to make their furniture. But, beginning around the late nineteenth century, recycled materials were commonly used.

The chest of drawers shown in photo 82, for example, was partly made from a large birch barrel. Because the curved staves were used to make the framing of the front of the carcase, as well as the drawer fronts, the front of the chest is dramatically curved in two different directions. Apparently, the chest was modeled partly after mass-produced examples of the era. It was originally painted white.

Like the chest of drawers shown in photo 82, the sideboard shown in photo 83 was made partly from unlikely recycled materials. In this example, the remains of a spool birch bed was used to provide the split pilasters flanking the cupboard doors, the spindles to support the shelf attached to the backboard, and the distinctive crowning section of the backboard.

The various recycled odds and ends from which the parlour sideboard shown in photo 84 was made, include legs from a large table, which were split and applied as decorations to flank the drawer and doors, and boards which had earlier formed part of a roof. Notice the traces of tar and tar paper which are clearly visible on the back of the drawer (photo 85). Considering that the sideboard was made for a formal parlour, the quality of materials comprising it suggests much about the economic circumstances of its original owner and maker.

Another example, the kitchen sideboard shown in photo 86 was improvised from the exceedingly rough timbers of a shipping crate (see photo 87). What appears to be a

82.
A late nineteenth century chest of drawers made partly from oak staves salvaged from a large barrel, collected in Spaniard's Bay, Conception Bay. Private collection.

83.
A circa 1900 refinished parlour sideboard of various woods including the remains of a mass-produced spool bed, collected in St. John's. Newfoundland Museum collection.

84.
A late nineteenth century parlour sideboard collected in Harbour Grace, Conception Bay. Newfoundland Museum Collection.

85.
Detail of the tar and tar paper on the back of the drawer.

86.
A late nineteenth century kitchen sideboard, collected in Harry's Harbour, Green Bay. Private collection.

87.
A view through a door in the sideboard revealing the rough packing case material from which it was built and the fact the item has no bottom or floor. Part of a stencil, "... HNS, N.F." (St. John's Newfoundland) can be seen on one of the boards.

long drawer over an enclosed cupboard, is actually a false drawer front. It is hinged and falls forward to allow the storage and retrieval of bread.

Even the exceptionally low grade of wood from which the sideboard was made, must have been difficult for its maker to obtain, considering that the sideboard doesn't have a bottom or floor. Furthermore, it appears that only one size of nails was available to him. On many interior and normally hidden surfaces their ends are flattened against the wood because they had passed completely through and stood proud (photo 88). Nevertheless, the quality of the materials used to make the sideboard is greatly compensated by the item's dramatically painted and carved decoration. The floral spray on the backboard, incidentally is both carved and painted (photo 89).

In addition to a shortage of good quality wood, the widespread practice of recycling in the outports was largely encouraged by the lop-sided arrangement which existed between fishing families and local merchants.[1] Until 1949, when Newfoundland and Labrador became Canada's tenth province, fishers obtained almost all their consumer goods from a local fish merchant by "truck" or "barter". A merchant would keep a record of fish received and items supplied in a ledger, and accounts were balanced up at the end of each fishing season. If the size of a fishing family's catch and/or the current market price of codfish were small, which was often the case, the family would be fortunate to break even, and they would have to be "carried" over the season. The end result of the barter system was that, for the most part, fishers were kept at subsistence levels, and during difficult periods, such as times of depression, for example, they often fell below.[2]

Considering the disadvantages of the barter system for fishers, it is easy to understand why outport people were highly motivated to make whatever they could for themselves from whatever materials were available and to make do with it as long as they could. They threw virtually nothing away, and when something wore out or became outdated, it was adapted to serve some new use.

Handy outport people used a variety of hand tools to make their furniture. Other tools sometimes included handmade treadle and hand-operated machines. An example of such a device is shown in photo 90. It was used by Kenneth Monks to make the fret-work for the bed shown in photo 120, and the wooden letters applied on the Gothic arch at the entrance to the chancel in St. James Anglican Church (photo 121). Occasionally, lathe work was simulated, using spoke shaves and even pocket knives as it was on the legs (photo 92) and towel rails (photo 93) of the washstand shown in photo 91. Other examples of such simulated carving can be seen on the parlour sideboard shown in photo 94.

Much handwork went into the making of this sideboard. Even the drawer and door pulls and the shelf supports are hand carved. The drawer and door pulls (photo 95) were modeled after commercially made examples similar to the imported ones on the chest of drawers shown in photo 32. While the shelf supports look like they have been shaped by a lathe, the type of turning they imitate appears to be inappropriate for the context in which they are used. The shape of the lower end of each shelf support resembles two turnip feet, one directly above the other. Normally, the shape of a single turnip was used

88.
Detail of the back of the hinged fake drawer front showing the ends of rusty wire nails bent flat against the boards.

89.
Detail of the carved and painted backboard.

90.
A late nineteenth century homemade foot-operated lathe and jig saw used by Kenneth Monks, King's Cove, Bonavista Bay. Newfoundland Museum collection.

91.
A nineteenth century pine washstand collected in Placentia Bay. Private collection. The original brown finish has been simulated.

92.
Detail of one of the hand carved legs.

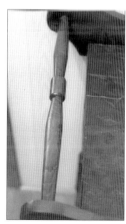

93.
Detail of one of the hand carved towel rails.

as a decorative foot on items of case furniture, tables and chairs. Other interesting details of this sideboard are the rectangular simulated panels carved on the drawer fronts. Their edges are chamferred in a similar manner to the door panels which are real. The ends of the sideboard are also worthy of notice. A rounded arch has been created on each end panel by the application of shaped sections of wood, and hand carved mouldings have been fixed around its inside edge. Short pieces of moulding were used to form the rounded section. Square nails are used in the construction. Incidentally, the over paint on the left hand drawer of this particular item was removed to expose the sideboard's original black finish.

Handy outport people, like practised outport furniture makers, patterned their furniture after British regional models. The late-surviving outport version of an Irish hanging dresser form shown in photo 96 is an example. The much earlier hanging dresser shown in photo 7, is the only other large hanging dresser of its type reported. Another example is the parlour sideboard shown in photo 97. This particular item displays strong Irish features from the South East of Ireland and County Cork. They include the beaded borders, applied lozenges (photo 98), scalloped decoration, and the shelf attached to the backboard.

As the nineteenth century progressed, the models employed by handy outport people, like those used by practised furniture makers, increased in number and variety, as eventually items of high-style and mass-produced furniture were used. One example is the table shown in photo 99. The pedestal of this table is hand carved to suggest lathe work; the marks of hand tools are clearly visible over the entire surface of the wood (photo 100). Interestingly, the table has no feet, and there is no evidence of it ever having any. The nails used are hand forged and the original mahogany finish has been simulated. Another example is the parlour couch shown in photo 101. This item is typically upholstered with

94.
A nineteenth century pine sideboard, collected in Harry's Harbour, Green Bay. Private collection.

95.
Detail of the left hand drawer pull.

96.
A late nineteenth or early twentieth century hanging dresser collected in Summerville, Bonavista Bay. Private collection.

97.
A mid nineteenth century pine sideboard, collected in Conception Bay, North Shore. Private collection.

98.
Detail of applied beaded decoration.

99.
A mid nineteenth century pine and birch plinth table of Regency inspiration, collected in Placentia Bay. Private collection.

100.
Detail of the pedestal.

painted sail cloth (heavy cotton duck). A third example is the kitchen couch shown in photo 102. Such couches, which were made for use in the kitchen, were typically not upholstered, and they were used primarily in addition to or instead of a settle to accommodate several people sitting at one time. This particular example was put together with forged nails and retains its original dark brown painted finish under several overcoats.

An unusual example of a homemade item patterned after a mass-produced object is the handmade frame shown in photo 103. It is modeled after similar looking examples decorated with four rosettes of moulded plaster, and made from material comprised of several layers of thin wood glued together and probably salvaged from a shipping box. The applied flowers which are used instead of plaster or gesso rosettes are hand carved. The photograph in the frame is of Mortimer J. Roach, and was taken in 1900 in Culls Harbour, Bonavista Bay. The frame was made by Mr. Roach, himself, according to a relative. However, writing on the back of the frame informs that the photograph was not put there until Sept 29, 1932. Presumably, the frame was made by Mr. Roach specifically for the photograph at this later time.

Homemade chairs were often patterned after factory-made chairs. Photo 104 shows two examples. A spoke shave was used to shape the spindles, back posts and legs of both. Notice the hand carved finials which were applied to the back posts of the rocker. Also notice the flat curving arms which are similar to those seen on early twentieth century mass-produced examples.

Like the initial models of British regional design, subsequently used models continued to be adapted in varying degrees in response to evolving conditions and the particular needs of individuals. When furniture was homemade, for instance, size, proportions and decorations were often adjusted to better suit new furniture for the contexts of the homes for which it was being built and/or to address a maker's level of skill, personal preferences and the materials with which he had to work. Perhaps not surprisingly, just as was the case for early outport furniture made by British-born woodworkers, and that made by practised outport furniture makers, elements from several different models were occasionally adapted

101.
A late nineteenth century pine and birch parlour couch enhanced with painted and stenciled decoration, collected in Clarke's Beach, Conception Bay. Private collection.

102.
A pine and birch kitchen couch collected in Bonavista, Bonavista Bay, circa 1870. Private collection.

103.
A handmade oval frame collected in Cull's Harbour, Bonavista Bay. Private collection.

104.
(Left) A small simple handmade chair of assorted woods, collected in Frenchman's Cove, Fortune Bay, early twentieth century. Private collection. (Right) An early twentieth century handmade child's rocking chair of birch, except for the oak arms, made in Ireland's Eye, Trinity Bay. Private collection.

and combined to make one piece of furniture. Very often, the different models were entirely unrelated in style, period or even specific function. Consider, for instance, the washstand shown in photo 105.

While the general form of this washstand was modeled after late nineteenth century factory-made examples, the small peg-like feet (photo 106) were copied from those employed on shop-made examples in the same area (see photos 49 and 52). As was mentioned earlier, this type of foot can be traced to rural Ireland, where furniture often sat on damp earthen floors. They were designed to be easily replaced when they succumbed to rot or were damaged. Interestingly, the shape of the harp is similar to that on the back of the washstand shown in photo 52.

Another example is the pine wall box shown in photo 107. Its general form imitates factory made furnishings of the Edwardian era, while the source of its decoration is most likely Ireland. The front of the box has a glass front and a hinged lid; the crest board and the skirt board are embellished with a flying wheel. The item retains its original brown painted finish, but has had a major repair to the skirt board. Notice that the hang hole is in the shape of a small diamond.

Yet another example of the use of several models, is the homemade potty chair shown in photo 108. It is flanked by two mass-produced chairs of a type which served as its models. The pattern of the chair back was taken from a "half-spindle-back" or "chicken coop" side chair, while the shape of the arms was borrowed from popular mass-produced rocking chairs of the day. It was made in Port de Grave, Conception Bay, from assorted woods, including tea box plywood material to form the box-like structure to hide the pot.

Perhaps the models used to make the sofa shown in photo 109 will not be immediately obvious. The item was partly patterned after a sofa and partly after a couch such as the one shown in photo 110, or a similar example. For an unknown reason, the right end of its shaped back has been sawn or cut away.

105.
A late nineteenth century washstand of assorted woods, collected in the North Shore of Conception Bay. Private collection.

106.
Detail of the peg-like feet.

107.
A practical and decorative pine wall box of the Edwardian era, collected in Conception Bay, North Shore. Private collection.

108.
An early twentieth century homemade potty chair, flanked by mass-produced items which suggest two of the sources of its design. Newfoundland Museum collection.

109.
A late nineteenth century pine sofa with birch legs, made by Andrew Young, a schooner captain who lived in Twillingate. Private collection.

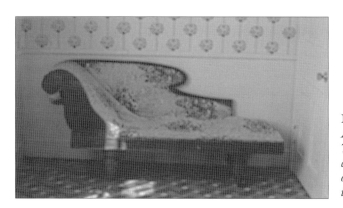

110.
A pine and birch couch made in Twillingate. Twillingate Museum collection. This couch, or a similar one, was used as a model to make the sofa shown in photo 109.

Another interesting example of adapting and combining elements of design from several models is the sideboard shown in photo 111. It was patterned generally after mass-produced examples of the 1900 era. However, much of its applied hand carved and gilded decoration, such as the gothic shamrocks in a vine format, was derived from traditional Irish sources. An Irish colleague, Matt McNulty, saw an Irish country case piece embellished with a similar motif in Kerry in the southwest of Ireland in recent years. The shamrocks were painted green against a warm yellow background.

A careful examination of the two ends of the sideboard reveals a puzzling feature: one end has three panels, while the other end has four (photo 112). But, there is a practical reason for it. The panels are not really panels at all, and the sideboard is almost entirely constructed from a shipping crate. Panelling was simulated by arranging and applying strips of wood over the boarded ends. The horizontal strips were placed so that they hid the seams between each board. Apparently, there were not enough boards sufficiently wide to create three evenly spaced simulated panels on each end. Therefore, on the end which had to have the extra board, it was necessary to apply an additional strip of wood to cover the additional seam which was created. The name, "John Hogan", is stencilled on the bottom of one of the half width drawers (see photo 113) . While John Hogan most likely is the maker of the sideboard, it is unlikely he printed his name on there. Presumably it was put there by the shipper of the packing crate from which the sideboard was made, to identify the individual to whom the contents of the crate were being sent.

The remarkable handmade washstand shown in photo 114 is an especially important and interesting example of adapting and combining elements of design. Its form is reminiscent of late nineteenth and early twentieth century mass-produced examples. However, elements of its design were inspired by both high-style and regional Irish models. The

111.
A late nineteenth century dining room sideboard, collected in Conception Bay, North Shore. Private collection.

112.
The end having four simulated panels.

113.
*The bottoms of the two half width drawers showing various
stenciled information and the name "John Hogan".*

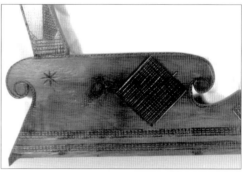

115.
Detail of the incised star.

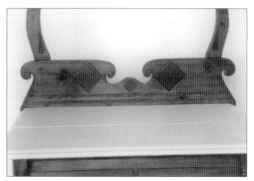

114.
*A late nineteenth century washstand
handmade from assorted woods and collected
in Conception Bay, North Shore. Private
collection.*

116.
Detail of the backboard.

carved decoration enhancing the backboard is the washstand's most significant and reveal-ing feature. The incised star motif (photo 115) forming part of this decoration is similar to that embellishing the chair shown in photo 9, and can be traced specifically to Southern Ireland. When of larger size, this motif is often enclosed within a circle and resembles a wheel. Also carved on the backboard are bands of hobnail carving (photo 116). This motif, like the incised star, also can be traced to southern Ireland. Hobnails, incidentally, were metal nails having raised heads, two rows of which were put around the rim of the soles of boots. The hobnail motif is also similar to patterns used to decorate cut glass, and Waterford and Cork were early glass-making areas. Another motif on the backboard — the diamonds filled in with hobnails (also photo 116) — can be traced very specifically to Waterford, Wexford and Kilkenny in Southeast Ireland. While most of the decorations on the backboard of the washstand can be linked to a specific Irish region, one embellish-ment was used generally throughout Britain. A close look at the backboard reveals that its edges are meticulously hand carved to resemble twisted rope. This type of edge decoration was used in the British Isles on good quality mahogany furniture and marble fireplaces. In Ireland, however, it was also used to enhance country furniture. The original colours of the washstand have been restored. The top was painted white perhaps to suggest marble.

The final example to be discussed is a most puzzling washstand. It is shown in photo 117. On first inspection, the washstand appears to be part of the ceremonial fur-nishings of a fraternal organization's meeting place. But, what group might it possibly have served? Each end, is enhanced with an applied arch of a type commonly seen on exteriors of Orange Lodges (photo 118). The Maltese cross, immediately above the arch, on the other hand, is a symbol used by the Society of United Fishermen, while the triangular shapes at the corners of the opening of the cupboard were employed by both organiza-tions (see photo 119). Furthermore, triangles also form part of the symbolic repertoire of the Christian Church, as do the crosses which are pierced in the triangles. To complicate matters even further, the type of chamfering on the moulding applied to the front of the washstand was popularly employed by Irish churches. Nineteenth century Irish churches also relied heavily upon applied and fretted decoration to enhance shrines, statues and a variety of other religious items. Though this bewildering cocktail of motifs is very puzzling, the mystery deepens even further.

Two details on the scalloped backboard of the washstand are of a less formal nature than those already discussed. The fretted flying wheel, for example, is a folk decoration employed, not only in the Celtic regions of Britain, but also in many areas of Europe. The carved motif which crowns the backboard is a related motif. Finally, the scalloped or sawtooth shapes which form an outline of two fish joined at the head, on the drawer front, is a folk decoration found on the exterior of outport houses, usually above the front door. As well, it has been used to embellish items of locally made furniture.

The variety of symbols and decorations are strange and bewildering bedfellows indeed, to find on one humble washstand. But, there really is no great mystery here. The washstand

117.
A late nineteenth century refinished washstand of assorted woods, collected in the general area of Port Rexton, Trinity Bay. Private collection.

118.
Arch applied to the exterior of an Orange Lodge.

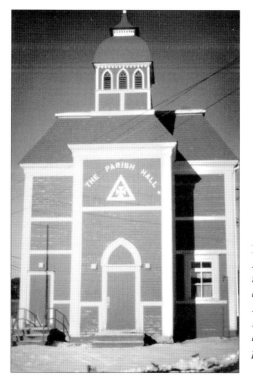

119.
Maltese cross within a triangle, applied to the exterior of the Parish Hall in Trinity, Trinity Bay. The building was earlier used as a meeting place for the Society of United Fishermen.

merely attests to the widespread outport practice of combining patterns from vastly different sources. The various motifs were chosen by the washstand's maker, simply because he thought they would look impressive together.

When first collected, incidentally, the towel rails of this washstand and their supports were missing. So were three of the four decorations which originally decorated the corners of the large diamond shaped opening of the unenclosed cupboard. These have all been replaced carefully following physical evidence visible on the washstand. Originally, the item was painted white.

Perhaps even more peculiar than the designs of the items discussed above, are those which included elements which were adapted and combined from objects other than pieces of domestic furniture. One example is the item which is still to be discussed and is shown in photo 132. Another is the remarkable bed shown in photo 120. This bed is generally patterned after iron and brass examples of the day. The Gothic arch and the fretwork decoration, however, were inspired by interior details of St. James Anglican Church in King's Cove. Kenneth Monks worked on the interior of St. James when he was only seventeen years old (photo 121). The construction of the church began on June 15, 1896. One of Mr. Monks' responsibilities was designing and cutting out the wooden lettering forming the quotation on the face of the arch surmounting the entrance to the chancel. To accomplish this task, he used his homemade treadle-operated lathe and fretwork machine (see photo 90). A similar style of lettering to that on the arch can be seen on a sign identifying the family's general store (photo 122). The bed was originally finished with a dark red stain. It has since been painted black and highlighted with brass-coloured metallic paint. An American print depicting the Lord's Prayer and the Ten Commandments is framed in the headboard (photo 123). The wooden finials, painted

120.
A birch bed made around 1896 by Kenneth Monks of King's Cove, Bonavista Bay. Newfoundland Museum collection.

121.
A Gothic arch, as well as quatrefoil and fretted designs, similar to those decorating the headboard of the bed, can be found in the interior of St. James Anglican Church in King's Cove.

123.
Detail of the framed print in the headboard made around 1896 by Kenneth Monks of King's Cove, Bonavista Bay. Newfoundland Museum collection.

122.
A sign used on the exterior of Monks' general store. Newfoundland Museum collection. The "K" originally appearing on the sign as a first letter, has been painted over and replaced with and "F" as the business eventually fell to Kenneth's son Frank and his son.

to resemble brass, are missing from the end posts. It is possible the bed was made as a wedding gift to give to his wife.

Like shop-made furniture, furniture made by handy outport people was usually designed using wood, cardboard, paper and even mental (from memory) templates, some of which had been passed down from previous generations of the makers' family. New templates, for the most part, were obtained from existing furniture in local churches, rectories, the houses of merchants and other important local people, and the homes of ordinary fishers. By the early twentieth century such furniture would have included early pieces made by British-born woodworkers, furniture crafted in local shops, locally made high-style and factory-produced items, British, American and Canadian imported pieces; and a vast variety of homemade creations.

Photo 124 shows a variety of templates which were originally made and used by Albert Rodgers, a Harbour Grace furniture maker discussed earlier. They are similar to ones made and used by outport people generally. At the rear are various templates for making table pedestals and legs. To the right of these is a set of templates for making applied rosettes. Directly underneath the rosette templates is one for making an applied case piece decoration. Other templates include a leg for a small tripod table, a shelf bracket, a spin top, a head for a toy horse, an applied split turning and a shaped apron for a case piece.

Apparently, some individuals took extreme measures to obtain templates for the furniture they wished to make. Around 1970, an elderly resident of New Harbour, Trinity

124.
Handmade wooden templates for making various furniture parts, circa 1900. Newfoundland Museum collection.

Bay, informed the author that years earlier his father ordered an entire dining room set advertised in an Eaton's mail order catalogue. When the set arrived at the local railway station, his father uncrated it, took measurements, made templates, and then unabashedly returned the furniture to the T. Eaton Company.

Like shop-made outport furniture and vernacular furniture made elsewhere, home-made outport furniture was normally painted, stained to resemble fine woods such as mahogany and walnut, or was grained. Very often, graining was of a decorative fanciful nature, and was not intended to simulate natural wood grain.

By the twentieth century, not all outport people pursued fishing as their principal way to earn a living, even though fishing continued to be the prime focus of economic activity.[3] Nor was it necessary for everyone to be as handy as it was in previous years. Nevertheless, many outport people continued to work with their hands and to make limited amounts of furniture. It was not only traditional to do so, the facility and the desire to engage in it was virtually in the blood. Consequently, furniture continued to be homemade, but for a variety of reasons. Consider, for example, the homemade potty chair discussed in chapter 14 and shown in photo 349. When this chair was made, factory-produced potty chairs and commodes of all levels of quality could be purchased relatively cheaply in the outports. Anyone making an item of furniture simply to save a little money, would not have lavished the degree of attention on it that this particular chair received. It was most likely made as a love token for an individual very special to the maker.

In the following chapters, the woodworking and furniture making activities of a selected number of handy twentieth century outport people will be looked at.

ENDNOTES

1. According to the late professor, Keith Matthews: "There were many sorts of merchants. Their role changed greatly between 1600 and 1830 and the smallest merchant — called dealers — by 1800 were often planters or fishermen as well. However, it is possible, I think, to define a fish merchant proper as he was in the early years of the nineteenth century. He was a man who owned his own seagoing vessels and possessed the capacity to import goods into his own stores in Newfoundland, and to export fish directly to the market abroad" [Matthews, Keith: *Lectures on the History of Newfoundland 1500–1830*, (Breakwater, 1988), 177].

2. Nevertheless, Matthews point out: "... settlement and fishing in Newfoundland depended absolutely upon the existence of merchants who alone possessed the money and shipping to import supplies and export fish. Without them the fishery must die, and the inhabitants starve." [Matthews, Keith: *Lectures on the History of Newfoundland 1500–1830*, 177].

3. At the turn of the twentieth century in Newfoundland and Labrador, three different fisheries — Inshore, Labrador Floater and Stationer, and Bank — were pursued. The inshore fishery was a small boat enterprise pursued by the entire family. Men did the actual fishing while women and children processed the fish on the shore. Families worked from their home communities. Families who pursued the Labrador Floater and Stationer fishery mostly were based in outports on the northeast coast of the island. Schooners set sail in June to take crews and families "down on the Labrador" to fish, either from the schooners themselves (the floater fishery), or from the land, where crews and/or families stayed in summer quarters (the Stationer fishery). The Bank fishery also was a schooner fishery based mainly on the south coast of the island. The communities of Grand Bank and Burin were two of its major centres. The Bank fishery operated from March to November and pursued offshore fish all the way from fishing banks of the south coast to Labrador. The schooners were operated by crews of local men and were equipped with dories, trawls and bait. Shore crews of men and women were hired to unload and process the fish.

CHAPTER 4

MR. WILLIAM WHEELER

Billy Wheeler (1891–1964), as he was referred to by members of his family and his community, lived in Keels, a tiny fishing village in Bonavista Bay. In 1983, when his furniture making activities were first investigated[1], the population of Keels was only around 135 people. Today, due almost entirely to the collapse of the cod fishery, the population is considerably smaller. More than half the residents have had to move away to seek employment in central Canada.

People who knew Wheeler remember him especially for his innovative fishing boat designs, not for the furniture he made. In fact, he made relatively few pieces of furniture during the course of his life, and the items he did make were mostly for his own personal use and for several of his neighbours. Nevertheless, according to many informants, Mr. Wheeler's knack for furniture making was just as impressive as his boat building skills. Mr. Fred Devereaux, a resident of Keels, commented: "He'd size up everything in his mind (rather than take measurements) and when he'd get it made it would be just the same as he had it sized up. He wouldn't have to change nothing." John Keough, a resident of nearby King's Cove, added: "No matter what Billy did it was perfect…."

Most of the furniture Billy Wheeler made was for his family home (photo 125) which was built by his father, Joseph Wheeler in the late nineteenth century. Wheeler inherited the house around 1917, when he was just a young man, and began to renovate and make new furniture for it. The renovations and the furniture he made are noteworthy for the way in which they were integrated and compliment one another. For example, outside the house, Wheeler carved lozenges or diamonds on the picket fence enclosing

125.
Mr. William Wheeler's house as it looked in the mid twentieth century.

the front garden (photo 126). He also included this motif as an embellishment on his front screen door (photo 125); on his parlour couch (photos 127 and 128) and on the frame of the pass-through from the kitchen to the back kitchen (photo 129).

Another motif — a shape resembling a keyhole — was used to decorate the stairwell (photo 130) and to enhance the door panels of a parlour sideboard which combines a late factory form with factory-inspired and Celtic decorations. It is shown in photo 131. He came up with a particularly innovative design for his kitchen settle which is shown in photo 132. The scrolled arms (photo 133), for example are reminiscent of those seen on fashionable English arm chairs of the Restoration period. The back, however, is patterned after early twentieth century church pews (see photo 134), and the open apron after chamferred muntin bars used in church windows (see photo 135). The use of shapes resembling muntin bars stems from the fact that Wheeler occasionally made and repaired church window frames. The settle is deep to allow for both sitting and lying down. The original brown painted finish has been simulated.

The way in which he embellished his kitchen couch (photo 136) was equally innovative. He employed a basically functional detail of the settle — the hand grip (photo 133) — to serve as a decoration on the face of the head rest (photo 137).

The majority of the furniture Wheeler made for his house was collected by the Newfoundland Museum following the death of his son, Jack. At this time of writing, the house is owned by an American couple who occasionally use it as a summer residence. In the author's opinion, the house and the furniture is a national treasure and should be preserved in context together for present-day and future generations of Canadians to enjoy. Hopefully, a serious effort will be made to do so.

ENDNOTES

1.   See Peddle, *The Forgotten Craftsmen*, 77–93.

126.
A section of the picket fence enclosing the front garden. The lozenges are carved in relief.

127.
A parlour couch made by Mr. William Wheeler. Newfoundland Museum collection.

128.
Detail showing the hand carved diamonds on the back of the couch.

129.
The pass-through in the kitchen, leading to the back kitchen. The washstand which is barely visible in the back porch doorway was also made by Wheeler.

130.
The keyhole motif decorating the stairwell.

131.
A parlour sideboard made by Mr. Wheeler.
Newfoundland Museum collection.

132.
A birch settle with fir seat, apron and stretchers,
made by Wheeler circa 1929. Newfoundland
Museum collection.

133.
Detail of the scrolled arms of Wheeler's settle.

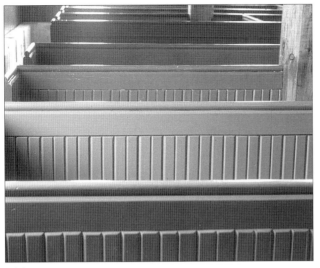

134.
A church pew in St. James, Anglican Church, King's Cove, Bonavista Bay.

135.
A window in the Church of the Immaculate Conception, Harbour Grace, Conception Bay.

136.
A kitchen couch made by Wheeler of assorted woods. Newfoundland Museum collection.

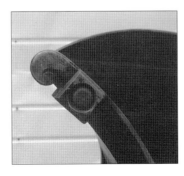

137.
Closeup of the carving on the face of the headrest of the couch.

CHAPTER 5

MR. WALTER BUGDEN

Walter Bugden[1] alluded to his passion for woodworking in his unpublished autobiography, "The Memories of Sixty Years":

> *The family were fisher-folk for generations: but if there be anything in inherited tendencies and tastes, some ancestor of ours must have been a worker in and lover of skilled handiwork; for it is seldom that a Bugden can be found who does not love to cut chips; and shipbuilding and house carpentry with much aspiring effort attest it.*

Mr. Bugden (1896–1946) was born in Petley, a small fishing community on Random Island in Trinity Bay. Although he was born into a fishing family, he never pursued fishing for a living. He taught school in several different outport communities for about 30 years; was a school supervisor and inspector for six years; and, following his retirement from that position, chose to become an Anglican priest.

While he was teaching at Eastport, Bonavista Bay, from 1890 until 1907, in addition to successfully meeting the numerous demands placed upon him as a teacher and as a highly respected community leader, he somehow found time to indulge his love for woodworking. In addition to constructing his own two-storey house overlooking Eastport beach, he also designed and assembled a number of choir seats and a baptismal font cover, which he donated to Holy Cross Church in that community in 1898. His most significant contribution to the furnishings of the church was an altar and reredos, pulpit (photo 138), bishop's chair (photo 139), litany desk and two prayer desks which he made from

138.
The oak pulpit made by Bugden, in Holy Cross Anglican Church, Eastport, Bonavista Bay.

139.
The oak Bishop's chair made by Bugden, in Holy Cross Anglican Church. The hand carving is enhanced by a textured background made using a small punch.

imported oak and installed in the church on the occasion of the completion of the Church's transept and chancel.

Following his retirement from teaching at Twillingate, Note Dame Bay, in 1915, Bugden returned to his birthplace of Petley and built another house for himself. As well, he constructed a large two-storey building, part of which he used as a workshop. During the next six years, while he worked as an inspector and supervisor of schools, he used his workshop to make a variety of church furnishings, much of which can still be seen in various Anglican churches throughout rural Newfoundland.

Bugden, however, made only several pieces of household furniture. One is the small bookcase shown in photo 140. Most of its framework is mortice and tenon joined. The end rails, however, are dowel-jointed to the stiles. It appears that some sections of paneling had originally been made for an entirely different piece of furniture, but were adapted for the bookcase. When not in use, the hinged writing leaf folds down, rather than up. Another item of domestic furniture Bugden made is the chair shown in photo 141. He made it for his daughter, the late Anne Sparkes. It has the initial "H" for "Hannah" neatly carved into the crest rail.

In an interview with Mrs. Sparkes before her death in 2001, she informed the author her father had not received any form of special training in the craft of furniture making, and he worked only with basic hand tools and treadle-operated machines.

ENDNOTE

1. See Peddle's article, "Newfoundland Craftsman, Part 1, Walter Bugden's life and work" in *Canadian Collector*, January 1986. Reprinted in *Newfoundland Quarterly*.

140.
A bookcase made by Bugden from various woods. Private collection.

141.
A birch and spruce chair made by Bugden for his daughter, Hannah. Private collection.

CHAPTER 6

MRS. ELIZABETH GALE

Mrs. Elizabeth Gale is one of Newfoundland and Labrador's most colourful furniture makers. What she accomplished during her incredibly productive life serves as an extraordinary example of outport ingenuity and creativity. Unfortunately, at this time of writing, she is confined to her bed most of the time. She has suffered a number of strokes and often does not recognize people once familiar to her. One of her daughters is caring for her at her home in Westport. (photo 142)

Mrs. Gale's granddaughter, Gail Collins, wrote an article about her for the *Women's Almanac* in 1992. She put it together by combining information she recorded from various interviews she had with her. Collins kindly allowed her article to be included in this book with the addition of several photographs she took of her grandmother and her work. The photographs were not part of the original article. They were selected by the author of this book to facilitate a more focused look at the furniture she made. Interestingly, the design of at least two items of Mrs. Gale's furniture comprise design elements adapted from several different models. The washstand shown in photo 143, for example, was patterned after both the washstand and the matching dresser of a late mass-produced bedroom set. Normally, lyre-shaped backs of mass-produced dressers held a swinging mirror; the backs of their matching washstands held a towel rail. The back of Mrs. Gale's washstand, however, is fitted with a mirror. The second item in which more than one model was employed is the medicine cabinet shown in photo 146. The hand carved decoration on this cabinet is a synthesis of designs adapted from circa 1900 mass-produced pressed wood clocks and a basket motif normally seen on hooked rugs, pillow cases and other linens.

142.
Mrs. Gale outside her home, busy at her cooper's mare.

Gail Collin's article begins with an outline of her grandmother's life.

Elizabeth Gale (nee Gavin) was born in Bear Cove, White Bay in 1910, into a family of 13 children. At age 18, she married Alexander Gale and moved to Pomley Cove, a nearby community of only a few families. While raising a family of four in this isolated Newfoundland outport, she not only performed the traditional female tasks of cooking, knitting, sewing, spinning, hooking mats, making sealskin boots, raising vegetables, tending livestock and drying fish, but also taught herself carpentry and furniture making. Using improvised tools and scraps of wood, she has made hundreds of items of folk furniture over a span of sixty years: everything from bureaus and couches to washstands and picture frames. She carved elaborate designs into most of her pieces, finding and outlet for self-expression in the decorative aspects of these very functional items. At the age of eighty-two, despite having had several strokes, she continues to live alone and make furniture, quilts and other handicrafts. Elizabeth Gale's life and work are profiled in a half-hour documentary film, Making the Most of Things, *which was directed by her granddaughter, Gail Collins, in 1991.*

"When I was a youngster they used to call me a tomboy because I was always going around with the hammer. If I wanted something done, I would do it, make a hen shed or a duck shed. I tried to make a spinning wheel one time and I partitioned off a bedroom for myself in my father's house when I was sixteen. My father wasn't a carpenter and neither was my husband, but they used to make herring barrels to pack their herring in to sell. Other than that I never saw anyone make anything.

143.
Mrs. Gale poses in her bedroom beside a washstand she made.

"I got married when I was eighteen and moved seven miles away from Bear Cove to my husband's home in Pomley Cove. My husband fished, worked in the woods and trapped in the fall for fur. There were only four families there then. We had four children, Maude, Arthur, Maria and Margaret. Maria died when she was eight years old. The bay was full of ice and we had no way to get to a doctor. The nearest hospital was at St. Anthony, hundreds of miles away. She took sick on the second of January and she died on the tenth. We had to carry her down to Westport to bury her. The dogs towed the coffin on a sled over the ice. There was nothing you could do.

"There wasn't much furniture in those days — just a table, chairs and a couch. In the bedroom you would just have a bed and a small table to put things on. You didn't have much clothes but what you did have you hung on hooks on the wall or kept in a trunk. There were no bureaus or dressers or anything like that.

"The first thing I made after I was married was a little chair for Maude. I thought if she had a chair she'd sit in the chair and she wouldn't be so much trouble. I had never made anything and I never seen anyone make anything, I just planned it in my mind and then made it. I had a saw, which was a piece of buck saw that I put a handle on myself, and a chisel, hammer and nails and a small plane. She liked the chair. She'd sit in it and she wouldn't let anyone else get in it.

"Next I made a washstand for my jug and basin set. I made it from pieces of wood that I found lying around. I didn't have a pattern but Mom had one so I made it from memory. When everyone was gone out I'd be at it and kept it stowed away until I had it made so no one would know what I was doing. When I made something I'd plan which way it had to go and then I'd do it. I wouldn't tell anyone until I was finished. I didn't want anyone watching me when I was making anything. So I didn't tell them until I had it finished and then I didn't mind them seeing it.

"The first bureau I saw, I made myself. I had never seen a real one. I didn't have a pattern or anything. I just looked in the Eaton's Catalogue. I used some pine Alex had sawed. He was looking for some logs to make some barrels and he saw this pine and he cut it because he knew I wanted to make something. He and another man cut it up into boards with the pit saw. Alex was away in the woods and when he came home I had it made and told him it was one I had come out of Eaton's Catalogue. He says, 'I know you had it come from Eaton's all right, that's the pine I had.' I said, 'Yes, that's what it is, I took the pine and made a bureau.'

"Well the first thing I had to clean it, make it smooth, then square it off, mark it fair, then saw it off, and carve it out. I made it out on the bridge. The children were small and didn't bother me. It took me a couple of weeks to make the first one. Before I had it nailed together when I was making it, I'd bring it in the house in the evening and poke it away somewhere. Then I'd carry it outdoors in the day on the bridge. I had it picked out in the catalogue a long, long time before I made it. It was easy to do, there wasn't much carving to the legs or anything, they were just plain. There was no carving on it, I did my own, carved it with a pocket knife. I carved a scroll design in the first one I did, after, when I made more, I got designs from old clocks and things to put on them.

"Everybody liked it when they saw it and wanted me to make one for them, then I'd have to make one for someone else. I sold them for $3.50 then. People would come from outside the Cove and they would see it and want one and then someone else would see that and they would want one. I think I made about 60 bureaus in all. I had to send to St. John's for varnish and the knobs to go on them and the glass that would go in it. I would order so much at a time and then I would have to wait until the coastal boat would bring that down, over two weeks from then. I would get the mirrors for sixty cents each.

"You wouldn't have much money in those days. You'd give your fish to the merchant and take up the worth of it in food and other things. If you had any left over they would want you to keep it on the books until the next spring. They didn't want to pay out any cash. But people would pay me cash for my furniture. I made washstands (see photos 143 and 144), bureaus, china cabinets, sewing boxes, couches, barrel chairs, picture frames and other things. People would write me and say what they wanted. I'd look in the catalogue and see the size, how big it was and I'd make it from that. I'd ship the furniture on the coastal boat or if it wasn't too far away, I'd put it in the boat and row it to the place. With the money I made I'd buy things for the home and material to sew clothes for the children. My husband thought it was hard work for me but I enjoyed it.

"Later on when I made picture frames (see photo 145), Alex would help me get wood. We'd take a rope and go into the woods on our snowshoes to cut down the dead pine. The dead pine is easier to cut because no sap or myrrh comes from it. We'd cut it into lengths we wanted then we'd tie it together and bring it out on our backs. I'd saw it out with the ripsaw. Rip it out the size I wanted, then carve them with a knife. I had stove out in the shed and I'd make them there. One winter I had an order from Roddicton for seventy frames of different sizes. People would buy pictures from people who were selling for Ryan's or other suppliers or take the covers off scribblers to frame.

"I never had many tools when I started. I had a piece of a bucksaw and I put a handle on it and used it for a hand saw. I used a picket knife for carving. And I had a square and a chisel and an axe and that is about it. Before I could get sandpaper I'd cut the tails off dogfish and let them dry and use them as sandpaper to smooth the wood. I'd use pieces of broken glass to smooth things off.

"I guess I started carving my furniture to make it look a little better. If I was making a sewing box (see photos 146 and 147) I'd use board that came from other old boxes that I'd take apart but I would have pine for the door, so I could cut the pattern. I marked it out and carved it on the cover of the sewing boxes. I got the scroll pattern from an old eight day clock. You'd make up your own patterns for furniture or for rugs. You'd double your paper once or twice then you'd cut it out to see what it looked like. That's how you made the patterns. Or you'd take a piece of coal from the stove when it would get cold and draw a hen or a duck or flowers or something like that for a mat. You'd take off a pattern from anywhere if you liked it, off a clock or off a dinner plate.

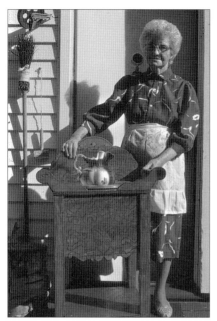

144.
Mrs. Gale shown standing outside her house beside one of the washstands she made.

146.
Mrs. Gale made sewing boxes which she sold for sixty cents each. She painted this particular example white and used it as a medicine cabinet in her bathroom. Her incised scroll designs were copied from circa 1900 pressed wood clocks; the incised basket of flowers on the door is a decorative motif commonly found embroidered on pillow cases and other linens.

145.
A pair of picture frames of the tramp art type, made by Mrs. Gale. Mrs. Gale would make frames in a variety of sizes and types to wholesale to local merchants.

147.
The cover of this particular box was made to hold a clock.

"My husband and I moved from Pomley Cove to Hampden in 1960, during resettlement. I didn't want to go but everyone else was moving and you'd be there alone with no one to help you haul up the boat or anything. We were the last ones to sign to move. You had to take your house with you, float it out, or build or buy a new one. I drew up the plan for my house in Hampden when we moved and my husband and I did most of the work on it. I helped to put the foundation down and put all the shores around and I was up on the roof when we put the main piece in and all the rafters. I had to go away for a couple of weeks to my daughters and they had it closed in when I came back but other than that I did all the work myself. I did all the inside work, putting the ceilings and the walls up and I put all the clapboard on outside. Before that I had put clapboard on houses in Pomley Cove and had done most of the work on our new house there. I renovated houses for other people too.

When I had the house finished inside I wanted cupboards so I started and built them in. Well after I had mine put in other people wanted me to build in theirs and I started and did that. I charged thirty five dollars and they supplied the material.

"There was always plenty to do in Pomley Cove. You'd keep animals: sheep, pigs, ducks and hens. You'd have to bring water for the animals from the brook. You'd grow your own vegetables and pick berries for jam. You also had to dry fish to sell it because there was no place to sell fresh fish. When I wasn't fishing myself I'd help my husband split his fish and salt it and spread it out on the flakes to dry. We'd sell it to a merchant who called around on his schooner in the fall of the year. I'd make furniture and hook mats in the winter and spin wool and make soap in the spring before the fishing season started.

"I fished for seven summers with another woman after my children were grown. We'd have a trawl moored. We'd pull up the boat every evening and push it off in the morning. We only had rowboats but the men had motors and could go out farther where there was more fish. We would haul the trawl every morning then bait it and haul it again the next morning. We'd go out in the evenings to jig. After you'd get in you'd split and clean your fish.

"I was thirteen years old when I learned how to spin wool. Then you'd have to knit socks and mitts and underwear for the whole family. I was 14 years old when I made my first dress. I got some material and I took a dress I had worn out and I cut it out by that. I made dresses for all my sisters after that. If you made a dress and it was a bit different to what someone else had, they'd be bringing you material to make a dress like yours. They didn't pay you but they might give you any material that was left over. I always made my own shoes and boots from skins until about the time I got married. When I got married I also made oilskins for my husband to wear in the woods. You'd make the coat and pants, then brush it with boiled linseed oil, then you'd press it out and hang to dry so it would be waterproof.

"I made a new spinning wheel the other winter. My son-in-law brought me an old one and asked me if I could repair it and replace the pieces that were lost. I started thinking about Mom's spinning wheel and I decided to make one for myself because there are none around like it any more. I just wanted one to see, to keep in memory of what was gone, so I made one near to the one my mother had.

"I really enjoy working, but I don't want anyone to know what I'm making because if I don't get it right and I get mad and throw it away, no one will know what I was trying to do. I'd rather be at my furniture than anything else, when everything goes right. I like to be doing things. I suppose it's grown into me now, and I can't get it out. It would be awful lonely if I just had to sit and study. I always have something handy that I can pick up and do. I don't want to be without working. I'm going to keep my fingers and hands busy as long as I'm able to." (photo 148)

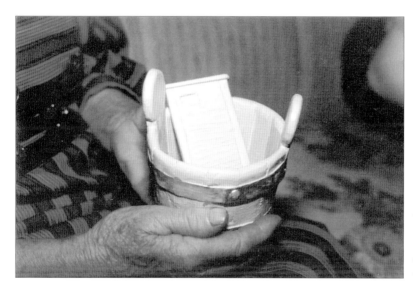

148.
Mrs. Gale holding a miniature washtub and scrubbing board she made.

CHAPTER 7

Mr. Clayton Ralph

Even today, at the dawning of the twenty-first century, some handy outport people continue to exercise their natural ability to work with wood and make items of household furniture. Mr. Clayton Ralph (photos 149 and 150), who was born in Port de Grave in 1920, is one of those people.

When he was just a young boy, Mr. Ralph left home to fish on the coast of Labrador. For most of his adult life, however, he worked as a skilled carpenter and house builder in various communities throughout Newfoundland and Labrador. Like many of his peers, over the course of his busy life, he built a number of fishing boats and made items of domestic furniture for himself and his family. When he retired from house building, he continued to busy himself in his workshop pursuing a variety of innovative woodworking projects, including furniture making.

Mr. Ralph's workshop is filled to capacity with the kinds and variety of objects which, until more recent years, could commonly be found in the workshops of outport fishers. They include numerous woodworking and fishing items, and many tools of a type normally used by various specialized tradesmen. For example, tucked in almost every nook and cranny are templates and patterns for making furniture, wheelbarrow wheels, horse cart shafts and fishing boats. Many of these tools, including several ingenious electrically driven devices, he made, himself. In an April, 1994 interview, Mr. Ralph commented about his father's and his own woodworking skills: "Whatever could be made out of wood, he could make, and everything I need out of wood, I can make it."

149.
A December 2001 photograph of Mr. Clayton Ralph standing beside the dining furniture he designed and built in 1974. While the furniture is of modern inspiration, he has added his own personal touches to it.

The following is an inventory of his workshop which was taken in 1994. It clearly reveals just how resourceful he is and attests to his astonishingly broad range of skills.

INVENTORY OF MR. CLAYTON RALPH'S WORKSHOP

Axes and Adzes
1 broad axe, nineteenth century
1 shipwright's adze, nineteenth century
10 hatchets, various sizes, twentieth century

Braces, Drill, Augers, etc.
1 auger/brace, nineteenth century
12 bits, auger, twentieth century
20 bits, auger, ship's, measuring from 17 inches to 2 feet, (43.3 cm to 60 cm), nineteenth century
2 augers, hand, nineteenth century
1 auger, ship or bear foot bit, twentieth century
2 borers, for putting shoulders on wheel spokes, nineteenth century
2 brace, hand, early twentieth century
2 drills, hand, first half, twentieth century

Chisels
1 morticing, nineteenth century
16 socket, twentieth century
1 tang, made by Mr. Ralph's uncle, from a file, twentieth century

Clamps, Vices and Wrenches
3 metal hand clamps, twentieth century
2 adjustable wooden hand clamps, nineteenth century
2 saw vices, early twentieth century
2 adjustable pipe wrenches, twentieth century
2 adjustable thumb wrenches, twentieth century

Files and Rasps
12 rat tail files, twentieth century
3 cross cut files, twentieth century
12 flat files and rasps, twentieth century

150.
A December 2001 photograph of Mr. Ralph in his workshop.

Hammers and Mallets

4 carpenter's, twentieth century

1 upholstery, magnetic, early twentieth century

1 tack, circa 1900

1 morticing mallet, handmade by Mr. Ralph, head enclosed with brass pipe, circa 1950

Hand planes

2 butt, metal, 1950s

2 jointer, metal, 1950s

1 jointer wooden, handmade, over 2 feet (60 cm) long, nineteenth century

2 jointer, wooden, over 2 feet (60 cm) long, nineteenth century

1 moulding, combination, Stanley 45, circa 1900

12 moulding, wooden, nineteenth century

1 rabbet, wooden, nineteenth century

1 sash, wooden, nineteenth century

1 smoothing, metal, Stanley, bought in U.S.A. in 1903 by Mr. Ralph's father

2 try, nineteenth century

Levels

1 metal, 1950s

1 wooden, late nineteenth century

1 wooden, mid twentieth century

Machines and devices made by Mr. Clayton Ralph

1 electrically driven grinder, 1940s

1 jig, for cutting tenons on the bed of his table saw, circa 1970

1 electrically driven lathe, circa 1970

1 electrically driven press and mortice-making machine, circa 1960

1 electrically driven sander, circa 1960

1 circular table saw with adjustable table, 1950s

Marking gauges

1 has double marking pin, nineteenth century

1 handmade by Mr. Clayton Ralph's father, circa 1900

Patterns for making furniture and boats etc.

Assorted furniture patterns for chair arms and legs, twentieth century

1 painter's grainer kit, 1940s

Assorted patterns for making wheelbarrow wheels, twentieth century

1 pattern for horse cart shaft, twentieth century

2 half hull models for speed boats, twentieth century

1 half hull model for fishing boat, nineteenth century

1 tap & die set, $^1/_4$ inch to $^1/_2$ inch, (6.35 mm to 12.7 mm), circa 1950

Saws

    Assorted circular saw blades

    1 buck, twentieth century

    2 compass or lock, twentieth century

    2 coping, 1960s

    7 cross cut, first half , twentieth century

    1 nail, (for cutting metal), twentieth century

    4 rip, first half, twentieth century

    1 tenon, nineteenth century

Miscellaneous

    2 mitre squares, circa 1940

    2 steel squares, twentieth century

    6 pairs of pliers, twentieth century

    1 tin snips, nineteenth century

    1 tin snips, twentieth century

    2 draw bars, twentieth century

    assorted paint and varnish brushes, twentieth century

    2 paint scrapers, twentieth century

    1 wire brush, twentieth century

    1 handmade brass plumb bob, 1950s

    1 metal plumb bob, nineteenth century

    1 oil can, nineteenth century

    2 oil cans, twentieth century

    1 grease gun, twentieth century

    1 moulding head for table saw, twentieth century

    2 saw sets, twentieth century

    1 steel for honing knives, twentieth century

    1 steel nineteenth century

    Assorted nail sets

    1 emery wheel dresser, twentieth century

    1 glue pot, nineteenth century

    Several mason's trowels, twentieth century

    1 sail maker's gauge, nineteenth century

    1 handmade twine pole for net mending, twentieth century

    1 handmade twine skeiner, nineteenth century

    1 handmade wooden hook made from a forked branch of a tree, twentieth century

CHAPTER 8

MR. RUPERT BATTEN

Further attesting to the view that the love and facility for working with the hands are in the Newfoundland blood are individuals like the late Mr. Rupert Batten (photo 151) and his nephew, Michael Smith (photo 152). Unlike Mr. Ralph and Mrs. Gale, Batten did not work during the barter system years. He was born in Bareneed, Conception Bay in 1942, and was only a boy when Newfoundland joined Canada in 1949. The author met Batten around 1970, and was a close friend and mentor until his untimely death in 2001, resulting from non Hodgkin's type lymphoma.

Batten's natural interest in and ability for woodworking was evident from an early age, and he began making items of furniture entirely on his own volition when he was eleven years old. During the waning months of the year 2000, he commented on the fruits of his initial efforts: "It was rough stuff and they (his parents) wouldn't let me bring it into the house".

151.
Rupert Batten (right) and his partner Frank Barrington setting up the Newfoundland Museum's travelling exhibit, Routes: Exploring The British Origins of Newfoundland Outport Furniture Design *in 1994.*

152.
Batten's nephew, Michael Smith, kneeling beside an unusually small circa 1900 outport chiffonnier he restored when he was sixteen years old. The photo was taken December of 2001.

Batten made his "first half decent thing" — an organ bench — when he was fourteen. He had been taking organ lessons from a woman living nearby, and the bench allowed him to more comfortably indulge his interest in playing the family pump organ and to practice his assignments.

Ironically, Batten's interest in restoring antique furniture was kindled after he had demolished a very old pine table which had been in his family's possession for generations. Batten had wanted to make a small table. So, in the traditional outport manner, he dismantled and reused the wood of the old table for this purpose. He reasoned that it had become rickety and was no longer being used in the house. Nevertheless, he had mixed feelings about doing it. Though Batten had a profound interest in and respect for "the old ways" of his culture, including recycling old objects to make new ones, he also had an equal interest and respect for the old objects, themselves. He commented to me in a somewhat sheepish manner: "It (the table he dismantled) had square tapering legs. It was probably a handmade Hepplewhite style table, and I destroyed it". Following the incident involving this table, he began repairing and restoring items of antique furniture. His initial projects were heirlooms that were either in use in his family home or stored in one of several of his family's outbuildings.

Batten never received formal training as a furniture restorer, or as any kind of fixer-upper, for that matter. In fact, in his early years, he had opportunity to pick up only very basic and general manual skills working with his father at simple tasks such as fencing and repairing farm-related equipment. It was only in his adult years, after he began working for the Newfoundland Museum, that Batten was able to acquire some wood working and furniture restoration knowledge from his colleague, Mr. Ralph Clemens (see chapter 9).

Rupert Batten has improved the health of and restored more pieces of outport furniture than any other person the author knows. His ability in this regard is as impressive as his interest in doing it. What he accomplished with the parlour sideboard shown in photo 97, for example, is almost miraculous.

Batten saved the sideboard virtually from the brink of total disintegration. It was collected during the late 1990s, by a mutual friend, somewhere in the general area of Conception Bay, North Shore. The item had been discarded and left to endure the ravages of the harsh Newfoundland climate. When it was first discovered, it was literally falling to pieces. In fact, some of its parts were so wet and deteriorated it was possible to push a finger completely through the wood. But, despite the fact it appeared beyond redemption, it was brought to Batten's workshop in Bareneed.

To prevent the slab doors and other vulnerable soggy parts from warping, Batten held them firmly flat with clamps. He then covered the entire sideboard with plastic wrap to facilitate the process of slow drying in his unheated workshop. The drying went on for over a period of several months during the spring and summer season. When it was completed, Batten fed the wood, which was partially decayed, with a mixture of glue and water. The simple concoction eventually hardened stabilizing and giving body to the wood. Batten also made new spindles to support the shelf fixed to the backboard; the original supports were missing. Finally, because the sideboard's finish was so deteriorated, and some of the wooden surface was so badly stained, he gave the sideboard a new grained finish.

In addition to making furniture and repairing and restoring antique items, Mr. Batten also developed a special interest in repairing the works and cases of old clocks. He commented: "It was probably only luck that I got them going at first". He attributes this particular interest to his great grandmother's brother, who, according to family tradition, was a whizz at making and repairing clocks. Batten's long deceased relative's surname was "Serrick", and he was born in Cupids, Conception Bay. His first name has been forgotten. During his adult years, Serrick travelled to Alaska to work in a gold mine, and later moved to Australia. Batten claimed he had a photograph of his talented relative holding two clocks, but he is unsure when and where it was taken.

Most of the antique furniture and clocks Batten has restored was done for the trade. In September of 1972, Batten opened an antiques store with the author. The business was located on the Battens' family land in Bareneed and was conducted in one of their outbuildings. "The Barn", as it was called, specialized in outport furniture and operated until 1976. During that time, Batten developed a glowing reputation for restoring antique furniture. In 1977, he was given a contract by the Historic Resources Division to restore a large number of pieces which had been selected to furnish the lighthouse at Cape Bonavista. This Provincial Historic Site was being restored to the 1870s period. About one year later, and soon after the author, himself, began working for the Newfoundland Museum, a job opening became available, and Mr. Batten was hired by the Historic Resources Division to work as a rough carpenter. His initial tasks involved helping with the renovations which were in progress at the Newfoundland Museum on Duckworth Street in St. John's. In May, 1983, Batten and the author each received an Award of Merit from the Canadian Museum Association in recognition of efforts to preserve outport furniture and to promote awareness of its cultural value. Until his untimely death in July of 2001, Batten continued to work for the Newfoundland Museum, as a Museum Technician responsible for building and maintaining exhibits. Restoration work, however, was not part of his Museum responsibilities. Batten also continued to repair items of outport furniture for himself and his friends.

Mr. Batten's nephew, Michael Smith (photo 152) was born in 1981. Like his uncle, has been demonstrating an intense interest in making and repairing items of outport furniture from an early age. Like his uncle, he too received virtually no initial encouragement or training. During his early teens, Michael spontaneously began acquiring woodworking and power tools and making small decorative wall shelves . His first serious project was making a Pembroke type table which he modeled after his uncle's late eighteenth century mahogany example. He was sixteen years of age at the time. Since the death of his uncle, he has regularly been called upon to repair items in the author's teaching collection of outport furniture. He currently attends College in St. John's where he is pursuing the study of mechanical engineering. The chiffonnier shown in photo 152, incidentally, was missing its backboard when it was collected in Dunfield, Trinity Bay. Michael designed and made a backboard for it using the one on the sideboard shown in photo 97 as a model. Two equally small outport chiffonniers are shown in photos 246 and 248.

The next individuals to be discussed, Mr. Ralph Clemens and Mr. Wm. Hilary Cook are examples of outport people who seized the opportunity to have their natural abilities honed by formal training. Mr. Clemens recently retired from the Newfoundland Museum in St. John's, Newfoundland, and Mr. Cook, from the Royal Ontario Museum in Toronto, Ontario.

CHAPTER 9

MR. RALPH CLEMENS

Surmounting family misfortune and an unpromising start in a tiny isolated outport community, Ralph Clemens (photo 153) became the province's most highly skilled cabinetmaker and furniture restorer of his day.[1] In the opinion of many who know him, Mr. Clemens' interest in his work goes far beyond technical concerns, and consider his attitude towards the furniture he works on to be almost mystical. In a 1986 interview with the author, Clemens remarked: "When I'm working on a piece of furniture that someone made, possibly 200 years ago, I feel like I'm an extension of that person prolonging the life of that piece."

Mr. Clemens was born in 1937 on Groais Island, a settlement of about twenty fishing families, on the eastern side of the Great Northern Peninsula. Growing up in such a small and relatively remote outport community during the years before Confederation was not a pleasant experience for many youngsters. For Clemens, it was particularly difficult When he was only three years old, his father died of pneumonia and his mother moved to St. John's to work as a domestic. Clemens, remained behind on the island with an uncle and aunt. When he was sixteen, his aunt died, making it necessary for him to haul up roots and move to the home of yet another aunt who lived in St. John's. This move initially caused him much emotional turmoil, but it eventually gave him the opportunity to explore a number of ways to indulge his love for working with his hands while, at the same time, acquiring new woodworking skills. Soon after his arrival at his new home, he set out on a path which eventually led to a challenging and satisfying career with the Newfoundland Museum.

His first step in that direction was securing a job with Newfoundland Hardwoods Ltd., where he learned to operate various machines to manufacture plywood. After about two

153.
A January 2002 photograph of Mr. Ralph Clemens in his workshop which is located in the basement of his house in St. John's.

years, he left this firm and enrolled in the Provincial Vocational Training School to pursue the study and practice of joinery. Following the required nine months of class-room study, he served his three-year apprenticeship with a small manufacturing firm, Benson Builders. Clemens, however, did not find the activities of his apprenticeship to be particularly stimulating. He commented: "we had to make more window frames than anything else". So, fighting boredom, he completed his apprenticeship in 1960 and worked briefly at the American military base in Argentia. Clemens' responsibility there was supervising a woodworking shop for hobbyists. The machinery and tools at his disposal allowed the making of anything from household furniture to small boats of the leisure class. But, it wasn't until approximately one year later, in 1961, that he landed a job that truly captured his interest. It was with R. Freimanis Ltd. in St. John's.

R. Freimanis Ltd. specialized in restoring and reproducing antique furniture. The business was owned and operated by a Latvian-trained cabinetmaker, Renie Freimanis. Freimanis gave Clemens the opportunity to receive his first training in cabinetmaking and furniture restoration.

During nine challenging years Clemens learned to make furniture in eighteenth and nineteenth century formal styles. He also learned restoration techniques from Leo Stoeterau, a German-trained cabinetmaker and fellow employee. Stoeterau had very definite ideas about how fine furniture should be restored. He insisted, for example, that an old finish should not be removed; it only should be cleaned and perhaps touched up. Furthermore, normal marks of wear on legs, rungs and stretchers of chairs and around the edges of tables and case pieces, should be retained. Stoeterau also taught Clemens how to simulate wear marks in appropriate places, especially on replaced parts, in order to simulate graceful aging and habitual use. To both Stoeterau's and Clemens' chagrin, however, the majority of Freimanis' customers wanted their antique furniture to look new. This made it necessary for them to remove old finishes and replace any parts which looked significantly worn.

In 1970, Freimanis moved to New Brunswick and opened a furniture factory. Though Clemens was invited to relocate with the business, he declined to do so. He preferred not to subject himself to the relatively tedious and repetitive process of mass-production. So instead, he took a job with the Historic Resources Division in St. John's. This allowed him to continue restoring antique furniture, if only on a limited basis. At that time, the Historic Resources Division was comprised of the Newfoundland Museum, the Provincial Archives, Provincial Historic Sites and the Exhibit Design Workshop where Clemens was stationed. Today, the workshop is managed directly by the Newfoundland Museum network.

Initially, Clemens' responsibilities involved doing a limited amount of general carpentry work, constructing exhibit cases and doing some finishing work. But, as the artifact collections of the Newfoundland Museum grew and more provincial historic sites were developed and furnished with period items, the need for restoration work increased. By 1975, Clemens worked principally on restoring furniture and heritage buildings.

Though Clemens' principal training and experience involved making and restoring fine furniture (see photos 154–156), his new responsibilities at the workshop included repairing and restoring the more rough and ready furniture of outport fishing families. He eventually developed a special interest in this work.

One item he especially enjoyed working on was the pine kitchen dresser shown in photo 24. The dresser had been found in a pitiful condition (photo 157), discarded on wet boggy ground near the edge of the road in Keels, Bonavista Bay. The original finish was

154.
Two Regency style mahogany chairs made by Ralph Clemens (1973) to compete a set for the dining room at Commissariat House, St. John's

155.
Mahogany secretary-bookcase showing Chippendale influence, made by Ralph Clemens (1980). Private collection.

156.
Pair of Hepplewhite style mahogany canopy beds made by Ralph Clemens (1978) for the Royal Suite, Government House, St. John's.

157.
A pine kitchen dresser shown before it was restored by Ralph Clemens. Photo 24 shows the dresser restored.

hidden by numerous layers of peeling over paint; a long wide strip had been sawn from the inner sides of each pilaster; and the shelf mouldings had been removed and thrown away. Clemens had the dresser brought to his workshop, and for a week he periodically studied, and analyzed its construction, finish and known history. He noticed that the top section had been altered, possibly around the beginning of the twentieth century, to accommodate a pair of doors. The alteration was most likely done to bring the dresser in line with the style of kitchen dressers of the day, which had glazed doors.

His discerning eyes also noticed fine grooves worn across one of the extending "ears" at the top of the dresser's base (photo 25). They had undoubtedly been made over a period of many nights by a fisherman mending his net. The constant relaxing and tightening of the twine during the knitting process had cut the grooves in the wood. Mending nets in the warmth of outport kitchens was commonly done during cold and inclement weather.

To determine the dresser's original finish, Clemens used a pocket knife to chip away tiny areas of the over paint in strategic places. Paint remover was not used for this particular task because it would have allowed the various colours of the overcoats to bleed onto the original finish and obscure it. Although Clemens discovered that the dresser initially had been painted blue and white, he was puzzled to find the bracket base had been painted orange. He surmised the orange paint was to match the colour of the baseboards in the kitchen into which it had been built.

While he was carefully removing the over paint with paint remover, Clemens observed that the door pulls were replacements, and that irregular gaps existed between each door jamb and frame. He deduced the gaps were made sometime after the original pulls had been removed and before the replacements were put on, by someone using a tool to pry open the doors. Finally, Clemens noted that the inside of the rack, or open shelf area, had originally been covered with wall paper. By the time the over paint was removed, Clemens knew the dresser sufficiently to begin its restoration.

Since retiring from the Newfoundland Museum in 1998, Mr. Clemens continues to enjoy repairing and restoring antique furniture, but only on a part time basis and for a relatively small number of clients. Most of the furniture that is brought to him is of the high-style variety. Clemens' son, Ralph junior, incidentally, works with a building developer as a finish carpenter.

ENDNOTE

1. See Peddle's article, "Newfoundland Craftsman, Part 2, Ralph Clemens' life and work", in *Canadian Collector*, March 1986. Reprinted in *Newfoundland Quarterly*.

CHAPTER 10

MR. HILARY COOK

Like Mr. Ralph Clemens, Mr. Hilary Cook's facility and love for woodworking led him to an interesting and challenging museum-related career.

Mr. Cook (photo 158) now lives in Ajax, Ontario, but he originally lived in Cartyville, which is located on the south shore of St. George's Bay on the west coast of the island of Newfoundland. He is the third generation of woodworkers in his family. His grandfather had come from Dorset, England in the mid nineteenth century and had settled on the south shore of St. George's Bay. According to Mr. Cook, he was a talented woodworker. Soon after his arrival in Newfoundland, he built his own house and made most of the furniture he needed to furnish it. Hilary Cook's father, William (photo 159), built himself a water mill and a small workshop on timberland he owned near Cartyville, and made a variety of domestic furniture items to satisfy the local market. The furniture he made included beds, chairs, tables, and kitchen cupboards; the woods he used included

158.
A contemporary snapshot of Mr. Hilary Cook sitting beside a spinning wheel he made in recent years. It was inspired by the earlier examples his father made in Cartyville.

159.
Mr. William Cook, Hilary's father, is shown testing the last spinning wheel he made. He is preparing wool while his wife is hand carding. The spinning wheel was sold to a vacationing American couple who had seen one of Mr. Cook's wheels on display in the window of the Nonia crafts shop in St. John's. They ordered it while in St. John's and picked it up in Cartyville as they motored home to Seattle, Washington.

birch, fir, spruce, and "balm", a relative of the aspen or linden tree which grows chiefly in river flats in the area. His father also did wood turning. He used two treadle lathes which he eventually harnessed to a small gasoline engine. In addition to making furniture and turning wood, he also did a little black smithing. This work, for the most part, involved tempering steel to make some of his cutting tools. About the time Hilary was born (1923), his father began making spinning wheels, and continued to do so until about 1958.

When Hilary Cook was a boy, he had much opportunity to observe and help his father in his workshop. As he grew older, his interest in woodworking increased and, eventually, he was able to take on his very own projects. Around 1946, Mr. Cook seized the opportunity to take cabinetmaking, woodcarving and design courses at the National Handicraft Centre at the King George V Institute in St. John's. After completing these classes, he continued working for himself until 1964. He then moved to Ontario to work for a yacht building firm. In 1971, he was hired as a cabinetmaker in the Exhibit Design Department of the Royal Ontario Museum in Toronto. He became foreman of that department in 1979 and held this position until he retired in 1989.

Mr. Cook's work with the ROM was varied. It was his responsibility, for instance, to maintain the good condition of travelling exhibits. These arrived at the ROM in a steady stream from many different countries around the world, and they were of considerable variety. Cook was also required to work on special projects. He remembers one particularly well. In 1977, the late King Baudouin and Queen Fabiola of Belgium visited the ROM, and the Board of Directors decided to present their royal visitors with a handmade silver item they were selling in the Museum Shop (photo 160). They did not, however, have a suitable box to put the gift in. "They approached me about it only a week before I had to design and make it", Mr. Cook commented in a letter sent to the author in 1998. "It was quite a rush job as it had to be made of maple to represent Canada and it had to have the ROM Logo carved on the cover. Anyway, somehow I got it made, but it wasn't as good as I would have liked (photos 161 and 162). The king asked to meet the man who made it so I got to meet them, and they seemed to be appreciative of it, so it didn't turn out too bad."

Since retiring from his position with the ROM, Mr. Cook continues to enjoy crafting interesting wooden objects such as the spinning wheel shown in photo 158. His talent and love for woodworking are shared by his two sons who are in the custom kitchen business. But, Mr. Cook is especially proud of his grandson, William Verne Cook, who is referred to as Verne. At this time of writing, Verne is 22 years of age, and works with his father, also called Verne, doing mostly house finishing and cabinet work. Young Verne represents the fifth generation of woodworkers in the family following his great, great grandfather's arrival in Newfoundland. Mr. Cook commented: "He has shown talent way beyond any I ever had". Furthermore, young Verne's skills are not limited to wood-working. He also has a gift for painting. Photo 163 shows William Verne Cook posing in the Gallery at the R.O.M. beside a chest he painted for use in a travelling exhibit. The chest was made by his grandfather, Hilary, and is a reproduction of an Egyptian clothes chest. Verne was only fifteen years of age at the time.

161.
The box shown closed.

160.
The late King Baudouin and Queen Fabiola of Belguim is shown in September 28, 1977 in the Chinese Gallery of the R.O.M. They are being presented with an engraved letter opener housed in a maple box which was custom made by Hilary Cook. The King was so impressed with the box, he asked to meet Mr. Cook.

162.
The box shown open and revealing the silver letter opener.

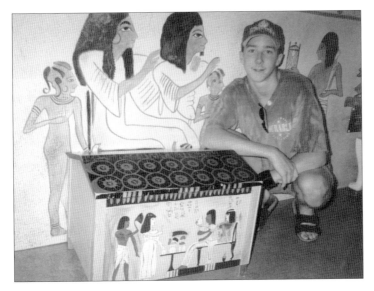

163.
William Verne Cook posing at the R.O.M. beside a reproduction of an Egyptian clothes chest he painted. He was only fifteen years of age at the time.

CHAPTER 11

THE OUTPORT HOUSE

Until around 1820, the majority of outport houses were single, two or three-roomed, single storied structures built from local timber. Exceedingly few early illustrations of the interiors of such dwellings exist, but published accounts of early visitors to Newfoundland indicate that these simple dwellings usually consisted of only a kitchen and several bedrooms. Furthermore, at very most, the furniture in them was limited to beds, blanket boxes, wall boxes and shelves, tables, benches, stools, and perhaps a few chairs. However, by the nineteenth century, the outport population had begun to increase significantly, and a sense of permanency had begun to grow amongst the local inhabitants. As a result, a larger two-storey house, which added a parlour to the original kitchen and bedroom plan, began to replace these smaller more primitive structures.

Photos 164 and 165 show a contemporary handmade model of a circa 1816 outport house. It includes the addition of a living room added at a later time and yet another addition made in 1850, to increase the size of the living room. The left side of the front of the house can be removed to reveal a clear view of the interior of that side (see photo 165). A large stone fireplace and kitchen can be seen on the first level, and bedrooms on the second. The miniature furniture it contains and its arrangement is purely speculative.

164.
The exterior view of a contemporary model of an outport house built in Bareneed, Conception Bay, in 1816.

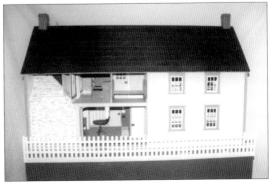

165.
An interior view of the left hand side of the model.

The model was made by Mr. Rupert Batten about 1995. The early house had been located on his family's property near the shoreline, and had been owned, if not made, by his ancestors. It is no longer standing, but the ruins of its rock foundation are still clearly visible. Batten made the model based on evidence he gleaned from the ruins and from older family members.

A house plan which continued to be commonly used until well into the twentieth century consisted of a back porch, kitchen and parlour or front room on the first level, and several bedrooms on the second. The back porch led directly to the kitchen and provided the everyday entrance. Occasionally, an extension of the back porch served as a "back kitchen". In addition to being used for the storage of foodstuffs and a variety of domestic items, back kitchens were employed for laundering and sometimes to consume meals away from the heat of the fireplace or the kitchen stove on warm summer days.

The front door of outport houses provided direct access to the stairs and often the parlour. However, because they were reserved for formal and special occasions, they were rarely used. Even today, those of many contemporary outport houses continue to be infrequently used and, as a result, houses of contemporary design are often built without steps leading to the front entrance (photo 166). They are eventually added however. The obvious lack of easy access to the front doors of many contemporary, newly built outport houses puzzles observant visitors, including even residents of St. John's, who refer to them as "mother-in-law doors".[1]

Until about the mid nineteenth century, many outport dwellings were heated by a stone fireplace which was located either in the end or near the centre of the house, and which opened into the kitchen. Some were the size of a small room, and their massive frameworks additionally functioned as a structural support for the two-storey houses. In addition to fireplace and cooking related tools, some large fireplaces were furnished with a pair of benches or settles which were placed on opposite ends against the stone walls.

Photo 167 shows one of a pair of such settles. Its higher end rested against the back wall, while the lower end permitted an unobstructed view of the kitchen. Sitting in this location also allowed an individual to keep watch over cooking food and to keep warm while performing various other chores. Furthermore, it provided a warm seat to accommodate visitors during various social gatherings.

It appears that stoves were not commonly used in the outports until relatively late in the nineteenth century. When they were, the stone fireplaces were eventually removed, sometimes leaving their stone foundation, or in others, a supporting wooden crib underneath the house. Photo 168 shows a mid nineteenth century house which originally had a large centrally located stone fireplace.

ENDNOTE

1. See Bill Callahan's column, "Now, the enduring mystery of the mother-in-law door", in the St. John's *Evening Telegram*, Friday August 14, 93, Page 3.

166.
A contemporary outport house, having no steps to the front door.

167.
An early nineteenth century pine settle having one end higher than the other, collected in Upper Island Cove, Conception Bay. Newfoundland Museum collection.

168.
A vertically studded mid nineteenth century house, Open Hall, Bonavista Bay.

CHAPTER 12

THE KITCHEN

Like early kitchens elsewhere in North America and many parts of Europe, the outport kitchen was the busiest and most public room of the house. In fact, it was so public and informal that community residents would enter one another's kitchen without the courtesy of first knocking on the door.

By the late nineteenth century, outport kitchen furniture was usually comprised of a mixture of factory made, shop-made and homemade pieces. Before or just after entering an outport kitchen, the first item of essential utilitarian furniture to be encountered was often a communal washstand. It would be located either just inside the back porch door (see photo 169) or just inside the kitchen door. A dresser was perhaps the most important and imposing item of kitchen furniture. It was used for the storage of cutlery and other utensils employed for the preparation of food, and to display both everyday and decorative dishes. Dressers were most often either homemade or handmade in a local shop.

Photo 170 shows a nineteenth century outport kitchen dresser which continued to be used in a traditional manner by the late Mr. Don Lear, in Hibb's Cove, Conception, Bay, until his death in 1993. The house in which it is shown was built during the late nineteenth century and retains much of its original furnishings. Judging by examples which have survived, until the late nineteenth century, the majority of outport dressers were of the "flat-to-the-wall" type and had open shelves. It appears that corner cupboards were much less frequently made. Furthermore, the majority of kitchen dressers, like the one shown in photo 170, were built as an integral part of the house.

169.
A homemade washstand photographed in the late 1970s in the back porch of an outport house in Rose Blanche.

170.
A nineteenth century outport pine dresser continuing to be used in a traditional manner in Port de Grave, Conception Bay.

Photo 171 shows another example of a dresser which was originally built into a kitchen. Because the right end rested against an adjoining wall, that end was not finished with a cornice moulding and the frieze was not enhanced with applied beading. The spaces between the open shelves are not evenly spaced. Like many dressers in Southern Ireland, the widest gap is located at the bottom to accommodate large platters, while the top shelf has the smallest, to hold a variety of tiny objects including small mugs and bowls. In this dresser, the gap is unusually narrow: it is only three inches deep. In southern Irish examples, this opening is normally no less than six.[1] The dresser was originally painted blue. The porcelain pulls are not original and the left hand drawer and the door are replacements. Boards have been added to the back to make the dresser free standing. A selection of Irish vernacular fascia boards is shown in photo 172. One is somewhat similar to the fascia board on this dresser.

Yet another example of a built-in kitchen dresser is shown in photo 173. It was photographed circa 1970 reposing outside Rupert Batten's workshop in Bareneed. The dresser has been stripped of its original blue/green painted finish, as well as numerous overcoats of paint. The decorative lozenges on the drawer fronts were carved there in relief; original ball and bail handles have been removed from them for cleaning. Because the dresser originally had no back, boards were added to the removable rack. Flanking the open shelves are, alternatively, small drawers and cupboards. The cupboards are enclosed with wooden covers resembling the fronts of the small drawers. The open base is a rare feature in outport dressers and facilitated the storage of relatively large items such as water and milk containers. The dresser is believed to have been removed to Ontario to serve as part of the furnishings of a museum or historic site near Thunder Bay.

The preference for built-in dressers in outport Newfoundland may have been partly due to a shortage of good quality building materials. Such dressers would have required less timber to construct, than would free standing ones. It is quite possible, for example, that the rack of the outport dresser of Dorset, England inspiration shown in photo 1 was built without backboards partly for this reason.

Hanging dressers and racks of Irish vernacular form were also made in the outports, but relatively few examples have been reported. Two such dressers already have been discussed and shown in photos 7 and 96. A much smaller example is shown in photo 174.

Other hanging dressers having glazed doors were also made. The example shown in photo 175 is most likely a handmade version of factory-made examples such as the one shown in photo 176. This particular item was made by the U.S. Moulding & Import Co., St. John's. Its original walnut finish and yellow line decoration has been simulated.

The majority of full length outport kitchen dressers having glazed doors date to the very late nineteenth and early twentieth century. The example shown in photo 177 was made by Frank Penny, a practiced furniture maker who lived in Keel's, Bonavista Bay. The front edge of the top of the base of this dresser is enhanced with nail head carving, an embellishment typically used by Mr. Penny. The shallowness of the dresser, as well as the "ears" extending out from the front corners of the top of the base, can be linked

172.
A collection of Irish vernacular fascia boards on display at Johnstown Castle near Wexford, in County Wexford, Ireland, includes an example similar to that on the outport dresser shown in photo 171.

171.
An early nineteenth century pine dresser of Irish vernacular inspiration, collected in Blackhead, Conception Bay. Private collection.

173.
A large early nineteenth century pine dresser collected in Cupid's, Conception Bay. Private collection.

174.
A small late nineteenth century hanging rack collected in the North Shore, Conception Bay. Private collection.

to Irish vernacular furniture design. Another more commonly seen type of dresser with glazed doors is the example shown in photo 178. One of the leaf carvings incised on its drawer fronts, for unknown reasons, was left unfinished (see photo 179).

Earlier nineteenth century dressers having glazed door were also made. One example is the dresser discussed earlier and shown in photo 30. Also made were examples having unusual features of design. For instance, when the doors of the dresser shown in photo 180 are open (photo 181), it can be seen that the rack is built in the same manner as racks of the open type, except for the addition of the doors. The dresser shown in photo 182 is of even more unusual design. It appears to be the top half of an early twentieth century kitchen dresser such as the one shown in photo 178. In fact, hooks from which to hang cups and pitchers or jugs can clearly be seen suspended from the bottom of the top shelf. The item, however, is a complete cupboard which was made to stand on the floor. It is made from various softwoods and the exterior was originally painted black. The interior retains its original coat of blue paint. When it was in use, the cupboard was stitched to the wall with nails because it was made without a back and was relatively unstable. It measures only 1.12 meters high.

Other forms of kitchen furniture also functioned to store and/or display food and food-related items. These include various versions of sideboards. An example already discussed is shown in photo 86. Another is shown in photo 183. This example has an opening enhanced with spindles in the high backboard, perhaps in place of a mirror. The example shown in photo 184 has a feature uncommonly found in outport pieces: a louvered door. The sideboard retains traces of its original red finish.

Small hanging wall boxes, especially those for holding cutlery (photos 185–190) were also commonly used. The tradition of using such boxes was most likely introduced by early settlers from Ireland. In Ireland, wall boxes and shelves were commonly employed to keep perishable items off damp earthen floors, and in some regions, cutlery was stored in a wall box only, not in a kitchen dresser.

175.
A late nineteenth century painted hanging cupboard with glazed doors, collected in Harry's Harbour, Green Bay. Private collection.

176.
A late nineteenth century hanging cupboard with glazed doors, made by the U.S. Moulding & Import Co., St. John's, collected in Open Hall, Bonavista Bay. Private collection.

178.
A circa 1900 refinished kitchen dresser of assorted woods collected in Bay de Verde, Conception Bay. Private collection.

177.
An unusually shallow late nineteenth century pine built-in kitchen dresser with sliding glazed doors, made by Frank Penny, in Keel's, Bonavista Bay. Newfoundland Museum collection.

179.
Detail of the carving on the drawer front.

180.
A circa 1900 kitchen dresser of assorted woods, collected in Plate Cove West, Bonavista Bay. Private collection.

181.
The dresser with the doors open.

The plain hanging wall box shown in photo 185 is typical of outport examples. Relatively few are as highly embellished as the one shown in photo 186. This particular wall box is decorated with a carved and painted heart and chip carving enhanced with contrasting colours. The chip carving is comprised of pointed shapes resembling the teeth of a saw. Similar chip carving was used to decorate the cover of the hat box shown in photo 344. Such shapes, incidentally, were created and employed in a variety of other ways. For example, a continuous line of projections resembling saw teeth was used to create decorative borders. See, for example, the washstand shown in photo 312. Round nails are used in the construction of the wall box.

Another highly embellished wall box is shown in photo 187. This particular item is of special significance. For its maker, the over-all carving on the surface of this remarkable box nostalgically recalls the Irish tradition of making utilitarian domestic items from flexible material such as straw and twigs. The use of such material stemmed from a crucial shortage of timber. In the general absence of wood, the Irish resorted to using rush, straw, willow and even turf to furnish their homes.[2] In particular, the inspiration for the latched wicker-like carving and the scalloping on the front of the box can be traced to country furniture in the west and southwest of Ireland. The embellishment of the front of the box is particularly innovative and complex. Notice that the partially pierced diamonds are cleverly carved to create the illusion that a straight edge, shaped to resemble a round sapling, can be seen through them. Also notice that, except for those on the backboard, the shape of the top half of the diamonds, which normally would be pointed, are formed by rounded scallops. The strategy of using a motif or design to serve more than one

182.
A most unusual early twentieth century kitchen cupboard with glazed doors, collected in Placentia Bay. Private collection.

183.
A circa 1900 kitchen sideboard of various softwoods, collected near New Chelsea, Trinity Bay. Private collection.

184.
A mid-nineteenth century pine food cupboard collected in Brigus, Conception Bay. Canadian Museum of Civilization, Culture Studies Division collection.

185.
A nineteenth century pine cutlery box retaining an old brown-painted finish, collected in Seldom, Fogo Island. Private collection.

186.
A circa 1900 cutlery box of assorted woods. Newfoundland Museum collection.

187.
An early nineteenth century painted cutlery box of balsam fir or pine, collected in the North Shore area of Conception Bay. Private collection.

purpose can be linked to the Irish need to economize space and materials. The box is put together with hand forged nails and retains a number of very old layers of scaling paint. The original finish appears to be yellow ochre.

It is the valued opinion of my Irish colleague, Matt McNulty, that the Irish influences on the wall hanging box shown in photo 188 are all slightly exaggerated. Nevertheless, the superbly chip carved and incised pattern and its style strongly link the box to Southeast Ireland. Residues of original green paint and later red paint are visible. Traces of relatively recent white paint can also be seen on carved areas.

The decoration on the hanging wall box shown in photo 189 may also be of Irish inspiration. Motifs such as hearts and flying wheels were commonly used to decorate furnishings in all the Celtic areas of Britain. In Ireland, however, due to a severe shortage of wood, these motifs were often formed by fretting and piercing. Such strategies required the taking away of existing wood, rather than having to add more on.[3]

Photo 190 shows a more rarely found three-tiered wall box. In this example, Celtic motifs are painted, their white colour contrasting with the dark reddish brown of the box.

Other types of cutlery boxes made in outport Newfoundland include examples which were designed to simply rest on a table, dresser or sideboard. The example shown in photo 191 is highly decorated, and the hand carved rope twist moulding especially, links it to Southern Ireland. Such mouldings were used, in most instances, to enhance high-style furniture. But, they were also commonly used by Irish carpenters to embellish softwood painted furniture. Rope twist mouldings were a nautical reference made popular beginning around 1800 by Nelson's naval victories.

The purpose of knife sharpening boxes (photos 192–194) was to clean and hone the blades of knives. The open box at the lower end of the long board was used merely to store a bath brick, rotten stone or other suitable material for this purpose. When being used, the knife sharpening box was placed flat, either on the kitchen table or on the working surface of the kitchen dresser. Knife blades were cleaned and honed on the long board. When it was not being used, the item was hung on the wall. The outport example shown in photo 192, though not closely similar to the Irish example shown in photo 193, has

188.
An early nineteenth century painted and chip carved pine cutlery box, collected in the North Shore of Conception Bay. Private collection.

189.
A nineteenth century painted pine cutlery box enhanced with pierced pan-Celtic motifs, collected in Bay Roberts, Conception Bay. Private collection.

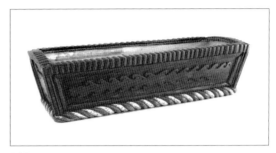

191.
A cutlery box enhanced with paint and carving. Newfoundland Museum collection.

190.
A nineteenth century three tiered pine wall box decorated with painted pan-Celtic motifs, collected in Bareneed, Conception Bay. Private collection.

192.
A late nineteenth century pine knife sharpening box, collected in Clarke's Beach, Conception Bay. Private collection.

193.
An Irish knife sharpening box on display at Johnstone Castle near Wexford in southern Ireland.

the usual characteristics in terms of size, shape and cutaway decoration, of Irish examples. The groove along the right edge of the board indicates the item was made from recycled tongue and groove lumber. The item shown in photo 194 is an untypical outport example. The front of the box at the bottom of the board is fitted with a sliding cover. A finger grip scooped from surface of the cover allows it to be lifted.

Other relatively late wall hanging boxes include comb boxes and soap boxes (photo 195). The source of their inspiration, unlike the various earlier boxes discussed above, was mass-produced metal and ceramic examples. These small boxes were hung in close proximity to a washstand.

The comb box shown in photo 196 is a rare carved example. The detail on the top front edge of the open box includes a series of shapes which appear to be the wide ends of hearts, but this is not the case. Outport people used several different kinds of edge and border decorations. These include scallops, sawteeth and dentils (see photos 311, 312 and 268), as well as several kinds of notching. Normally each of such shapes was produced in a series with equal gaps between them. But in the outports, they are occasionally found in unusual contexts and combinations, and they are sometimes formed in unusual ways. On the edge of this comb box, for example, a series of dentils is combined with simple notches most likely shaped with a hand file. Because one notch is cut in the centre of the top forward edge of each dentil, the illusion of a roughly-shaped heart motif is created. Furthermore, the dentils are not cut completely through the edge of the wood, but are carved on the forward edge. The gaps between them are flat beveled surfaces which somewhat resemble mirror reflections of the dentils. A close look will reveal that a notch is also cut in the centre of the top forward edge of these gaps. In three of them, a shape somewhat resembling the sawtooth shape on the drawer fronts of the chest shown in photo 337 , are carved. Other similar ingenious combinations of scallops, sawteeth and dentils can be seen in photos 269, 271 and 337. These items, as well as the comb box, were most likely made by the same person.

The small punched holes bordering the pierced motifs and creating a vague design on the back tablet of the comb box, may have been used to suggest seeds — a symbol for fertility (see a similar decoration on the washstand shown in photo 73). The relatively large back tablet, incidentally, is most likely in imitation of mass-produced metal examples. When the reverse side of the comb box is examined (photo 197), it will be seen that the item was made from boards salvaged from a used Sunlight Soap shipping crate. The original blue paint has been simulated.

In addition to wall boxes, shelves were commonly used to hold a variety of decorative and utilitarian objects (photos 198 and 199). The example shown in photo 199 is highly derived from Irish vernacular tradition. Some of its edges are embellished with a series of circle segments or scallops; others with a series of angular projections which resemble the teeth of a saw. Scalloping and saw teeth are combined on the top edge of the backboard. Such decoration was a simple way to liven up the edges of wood and to create borders when only simple hand tools were available. Like fretting, such decoration normally

194.
An unusually designed late nineteenth century pine knife sharpening box, collected in Dunfield, Trinity Bay. Private collection.

195.
Left to right: a circa 1900 pine comb box, soap box and comb box collected in the Bonavista Peninsula area. Private collection.

196.
A circa 1900 comb box embellished with chip carving and punched and fretted motifs, collected in the North Shore, Conception Bay. Private collection.

197.
The reverse side of the comb box, revealing it was made from wood salvaged from a Sunlight Soap packing crate.

198.
A late nineteenth century painted pine wall shelf, collected in the Bonavista Peninsula. Private collection.

199.
A late nineteenth century wall shelf retaining its original dark stained finish, collected in Old Bonaventure, Trinity Bay. Private collection.

required the taking away of wood, rather than having to add it on, a decided advantage in Ireland where there was a serious shortage of timber. The way in which the two ends of the shelf were made also reflect the Irish need to economize both time and materials. The edges of a single board was shaped and split in half to make the two ends. This practice also ensured that the two ends would be virtually identical in appearance.

A homemade, shop-made or factory-made drop leaf table was the most commonly used type for the consumption of meals. Most, like the ones shown in photos 200 and 202, have two drop leaves. The example shown in photo 200 is unusually embellished with small quarter turned applied split spindles (photo 201) in a place that normally would be difficult to see: the top of the legs.

Some tables, had only one leaf, and some, like the table shown in photo 203, had no leaves at all. The crackled finish on the legs and apron of this table is the original. The top, which had been unfinished, has recently been painted brown to protect it and to match the colour of the finish on the rest of the table. One of its most interesting features is its apron which is scrolled on all four sides. At some time during its lifetime, someone has slightly rounded each of four corners of the table top. Another large kitchen table which was made without leaves is shown in photo 204. Its legs were shaped with a hand tool, and forged nails were used in its construction.

Smaller tables served a variety of purposes in the kitchen, such as preparing food and accomplishing a wide range of other tasks. They were even used for leisurely pursuits. The example shown in photo 205 has a top apron which is generously enhanced with applied moulding. Notice how similar in appearance it is to that of the washstand shown in photo 308. Forged nails are used in its construction. Another example, shown in

200.
A nineteenth century pine and birch painted drop leaf table with stout turned legs, collected in the North Shore, Conception Bay. Private collection.

201.
Detail of the applied decoration at the top of the legs.

202.
A nineteenth century pine and birch drop leaf table retaining much of its original boldly grained finish, collected in Conception Bay, North Shore. Private collection.

203.
A nineteenth century pine and birch table collected in King's Point, Green Bay. Private collection.

204.
A circa 1870 stretcher table made entirely of pine and collected in Angel's Cove, Cape Shore. Private collection.

205.
A nineteenth century pine table of eighteenth century vernacular persuasion, retaining much of its original painted finish, as well as several overcoats of old paint, collected in the Seldom, Fogo Island. Private collection.

photo 206, has a sawtooth embellishment on the backboard. This is a detail commonly found on tables made in the Conception Bay North Shore area. It was, however, used throughout the outports generally, often in combination with various other forms of scalloping, as an edge decoration (see, for example, the pine wall shelf in photo 199). The corners of the apron of the table shown in photo 207 are mitred. However, mortice and tenon joints are used in the construction of the stretcher. A similar construction strategy was employed in rural Ireland. Perhaps the most interesting example of a small kitchen table is shown in photo 208. The heart and fan motifs enhancing its chip-carved top (photo 209) link it to southern Ireland. A most unusual detail is the chip carving on the top end of each of the legs. These ends come through the table top to form through tenons. Notice that the stylized flower motif on three of them have only four leaves, while one has six. Presumably, the one having six (photo 210) was carved first. The more simplified version on the others was a result of the maker having difficulty working on end grain.

The earliest major form of kitchen seating is the settle. These items were usually placed just to one side or directly opposite the kitchen fire place or stove. In addition to seating several people at one time, they were employed, especially by the man of the house, to lie upon and steal a few winks. The majority of examples reported have low backs and are of two basic types. One type is comprised of horizontally oriented boards and is similar to examples made throughout Britain generally. The example shown in photo 211 was photographed in the kitchen of the house for which it was made, in Port de Grave, Conception Bay. The wide end of a heart is cut from both the top edge of the back and the bottom edge of the apron perhaps to compliment the heart carved on the back of

206.
A late nineteenth century refinished pine table, collected in Kingston, Conception Bay. Newfoundland Museum collection.

207.
A nineteenth century painted pine table of Irish vernacular influence, collected in Bay Roberts, Conception Bay. Private collection.

208.
A nineteenth century pine chip-carved games table, collected in St. John's, but reputed to have been brought there from central Newfoundland. Newfoundland Museum collection.

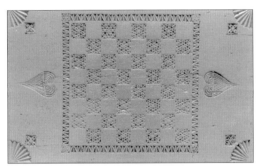

209.
The top of the chip carved games table.

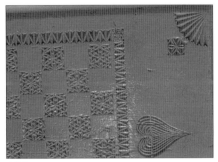

210.
Detail showing the six-pointed stylized flower motif.

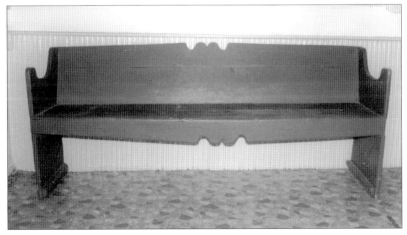

211.
A late nineteenth century painted pine settle, photographed in the kitchen of the house for which it was made.

the couch used in the same room (photo 221) and the wide end of a heart employed in an upside down position on the apron of a painted washstand used in an upstairs bedroom (photo 306). The second example, which is shown in photo 212, is unusually small and has drawers constructed in its apron. Some of the tongue and groove boards from which it was constructed were cut almost diagonally across the grain, suggesting there was an acute shortage of suitable building material at the time of its making. Several similar, but longer, settles having drawers have been reported.

Unlike these settles, the other type has an open back and arms. The back and sometimes the arms are enhanced with rounded or flat spindles. The example shown in photo 213 retains its original reddish-brown painted finish, and its seat is comprised of a single board. The one shown in photo 214 retains many old layers of dried and crumbling paint. It was donated to the Newfoundland Museum by Mr. Lloyd George, and was made by one of his forebears who had emigrated from Wales. Unlike the vast majority of settles made in the outports, the example shown in photo 215 has an unusually narrow seat. At some time in its life, it was widened, perhaps to permit reclining upon it. In recent years, the seat was restored to its original size by Rupert Batten. The construction includes through mortice and tenon joints, and the original black finish is covered by old brown paint. The alternating saw tooth and scooped scallops on the rail edges (photo 216) and the edges of the apron, as well as the item's shallow depth, suggest an Irish influence.

In addition to the two kinds of settles described above, a relatively small number were made having paneled backs. Others, like the example shown in photo 217, are one-of-a-kind homemade items. This example has unusual curved and partially open ends; its wavy back is most likely of Irish vernacular persuasion. To the author's knowledge, no solid board examples have been reported which have high backs comprised of vertically oriented boards, similar to ones made in the English West Country.

212.
A late nineteenth century painted settle made from assorted woods, collected in Spaniard's Bay, Conception Bay. Private collection.

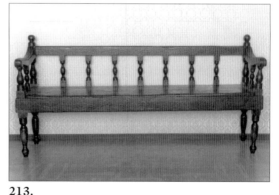

213.
A nineteenth century pine and birch baluster-back settle, collected in Bay Roberts, Conception Bay. Private collection.

214.
A nineteenth century turned settle collected in Dildo, Trinity Bay. Newfoundland Museum collection.

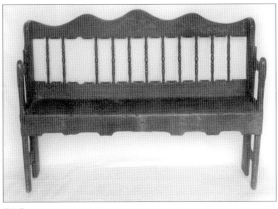

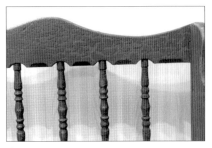

216.
Detail of the edge decoration on the back rails.

215.
A nineteenth century pine and birch spindle-back settle, collected in Clarke's Beach, Conception Bay. Private collection.

217.
A nineteenth century painted pine and birch settle collected in Keels, Bonavista Bay. Private collection.

Although settles were made in the outports until well into the twentieth century, by the mid nineteenth century informal handmade versions of the high-style sofa and the high-style couch began to make their appearance in outport kitchens. Unlike those made for the parlour, however, kitchen examples were almost never upholstered. Instead, their solid plank seats were usually covered with a removable pad. Like settles, kitchen sofas and couches were used both to sit and to recline upon.

The example shown in photo 218 is an interesting combination of formal regency form and informal Irish embellishment. Except for the apron and legs, which are birch, the sofa is made of pine. Pegged mortice and tenon joints are used in the construction, and wooden pegs, rather than nails, are employed to hold the seat to its frame. The original red paint is covered with a subsequent overcoat of red, and the original yellow line decoration has been reinforced with fresh paint. The board forming the seat of the more simply designed kitchen sofa shown in photo 219 has boards which run from front to back. Presumably, this strategy resulted in a sturdier seat than that provided by the more common method of horizontal orientation.

The innovatively designed kitchen couch shown in photo 220 has a scalloped back which has been subtly adapted to suggest ocean waves. Scalloping is also applied to each end of the apron to suggest the wide end of a heart in a horizontal position. The example shown in photo 221 has a carved heart centred on its back (photo 222). This motif was adapted to enhance several other items of furniture used in the same house. For example, a portion of a heart motif is cut into the back and apron of a settle used in the same kitchen (photo 211), and employed in an upside down position on the front and side aprons of a washstand used in one of the bedrooms (photo 306).

Kitchen sofas and couches did not necessarily replace settles as the major form of outport kitchen seating. In some instances, they were used in addition to a settle (see, for example, photos 211 and 221 for a settle and couch used in the same kitchen). In fact, in some respects, kitchen sofas and couches are actually settles masquerading as

218.
A circa 1840 kitchen sofa collected in Port Rexton, Trinity Bay. Private collection.

219.
A nineteenth century pine and birch kitchen sofa collected in Bonavista, Bonavista Bay. Canadian Museum of Civilization, Culture Studies Division collection.

220.
A late nineteenth century pine and spruce kitchen couch collected in Keels Bonavista Bay. Private collection.

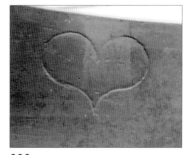

222.
Detail of the heart carved on the back of the couch.

221.
A late nineteenth century pine and birch kitchen couch photographed outside the kitchen of the house for which it was made.

their high-style cousins. Supporting this view are many large outport seating forms which appear to be a combination of either settle and couch, or settle and sofa design.

One unusual example is the homemade settle shown in photo 223. It was photographed sometime during the late 1980s along with several other items of painted furniture which were removed from a house in Plate Cove East, Bonavista Bay, to facilitate renovating and painting the house. Its form is clearly a combination of that of a traditional solid board settle and that of a couch. The form of the example shown in photo 224, on the other hand, was partly influenced by that of a sofa.

Perhaps not surprisingly, wooden versions of mass-produced cots were also handmade in outport Newfoundland. But all examples reported are most likely one-of-a-kind homemade items. There is no evidence to indicate any were shop-made for the outport domestic furniture market. The painted couch shown in photo 225 is an example. It was patterned partly after a mass-produced metal folding cot, and was made circa 1900, of various woods. The seat and back were originally covered with painted sail cloth and stuffed with straw. The bench shown in photo 226 was also patterned after a mass-produced cot. It too was made of assorted woods circa 1900. Like settles, it too was used for sitting and reclining upon. The head rest at one end is formed by a raised and slightly sloping platform enclosed on three sides by a low gallery. The stretchers are joined to the legs by through mortice and tenon joints. The bench has been refinished; it was originally painted red. The item shown in photo 227 was partly patterned after this bench and partly after a kitchen couch. Both items were most likely made by the same individual. The decoration incised on the applied detail on the back (photo 228) may be a distorted interpretation of an incised star, an embellishment which can be traced to South East Ireland (see photo 9).

223.
A 1980s photograph of painted furniture, including an unusual settle, removed from a house in Plate Cove East, Bonavista Bay, to facilitate renovating and painting the house.

224.
A circa 1870 pine and birch painted settle, photographed in Conche on the Great Northern Peninsula.

225.
A circa 1900 painted wooden couch of various woods, partly patterned after a mass-produced metal folding cot, collected in Marysvale, Conception Bay. Private collection.

226.
A circa 1900 bench of assorted woods, patterned after a mass-produced cot, collected in Conception Bay, North Shore. Private collection.

228.
Detail of the incised carving on the back of the couch.

227.
A circa 1900 couch partly patterned after the bench shown in photo 226 and partly after a kitchen couch, collected in the North Shore, Conception Bay. Private collection.

Benches, stools and chairs of many kinds were made in the outports for use in the kitchen. The three-legged low stool shown in photo 229 is the only outport example of its type reported. Such stools were commonly used in Ireland and Scotland, for sitting near the fire. They helped to keep the sitter's head below the smoke line and were referred to as "creepies". The seat frame of this example is comprised of a "V"-shaped natural growth of birch (photo 230). The three legs are socketed into the frame, and the boards forming the seat are fixed to it with forged nails. The stretchers connecting the ends of the stool shown in photo 231 are uncommon in outport furniture. Forged nails are used in its construction. The example shown in photo 232 is enhanced on each apron with a fretted diamond with drilled corners. The colour of its original paint appears to be brown.

As already shown, many early outport chairs were modeled after a variety of Irish regional examples. It appears they were less frequently patterned after chairs of other British regions. Perhaps the most commonly found examples of English regional inspiration are turned spindle back chairs. An example already discussed is shown in photo 8. Another can be seen in photo 233. The decorative ball turnings on the three back spindles of this particular chair are flattened on the forward side. Forged nails were used to hold the pine seat to its frame. The chair has been stripped of its numerous layers of paint. The example shown in photo 234 is very similar in form to a local example having arms and shown in *The Early Furniture of Ontario & the Atlantic Provinces*, Henry and Barbara Dobson, M.F. Feheley Publishers Co. Limited, 1974. The feet on this chair, however, show significant wear, and most likely have been shortened. Furthermore, the turned top and bottom rails which hold the spindles forming part of the back have been shaped to simulate bamboo, and the chair has been refinished.

While some chairs of the early Windsor type were homemade in the outports, it seems few were shop-produced. Only several skillfully crafted examples, similar to Windsor chairs commonly made in Cornwall and Devon during the first half of the nineteenth century, have been reported. However, it is not known whether these particular chairs were made

229.
An early nineteenth century pine "creepie" collected in Marysvale, Conception Bay. Private collection.

230.
The underside of the creepie showing the frame of naturally shaped wood.

231.
A sturdy nineteenth century painted pine stool or bench collected in the Placentia Bay area. Private collection.

232.
A nineteenth century pine stool enhanced on each apron with a fretted diamond with drilled corners, collected in Conception Bay North. Private collection.

233.
One of a pair of circa 1800 pine and birch turned chairs collected in Brigus, Conception Bay. Canadian Museum of Civilization, Culture Studies Division collection.

234.
An early nineteenth century pine and birch turned chair, collected in Carbonear, Conception Bay. Private collection.

in England using some Newfoundland timber, or were made in Newfoundland using some English-grown woods. Only the ash 'hoop' and stretchers and the elm seats of examples found in Newfoundland conform to West Country examples.[4] The legs and spindles are birch. An example is shown in photo 235.

A relatively small number of chairs having front legs made from naturally-shaped wood, similar to boat knees, were made throughout the nineteenth and early twentieth century (photos 236, 348 and 296). Each "knee" would form one leg and one side of the seat frame (photo 237). The stiles and each spindle of the example shown in photo 236 are fixed to the crest rail with wooden pins. The birch plank seat is fastened to the seat frame in the same manner. Other construction details include through socket joints to hold the stretchers to the legs. The chair retains residues of its original blue painted finish underneath several overcoats of brown paint. Other examples are shown in photos 348 and 296.

Naturally-shaped wood was employed for other essential components of chairs as well. The chair shown in photo 238, for example, has flat armrests which are made from two naturally-shaped pieces of wood. They are lapped at the rear. The four stiles which support these curved armrests and the seat are also naturally-shaped. The chair is made from assorted woods including birch, and its various components were held together with screws. The use of naturally-shaped wood to make furniture and other objects, incidentally, was not peculiar to the traditions of any one specific British region. Rural cultures generally, especially those being in close proximity to the sea, indulged in this practice.

A commonly made chair during the nineteenth and early twentieth century were simple adult's and child's chairs of solid board construction. The example shown in photo 239 was made from a shipping box and painted red. Its style has a decidedly Irish flavour. Interestingly, it was a common practice in Ireland, just as it was in Newfoundland and Labrador, to use shipping boxes to make furniture. In Ireland, such material was especially popular for making children's furniture.

235.
A circa 1820 Windsor chair collected in Newfoundland. Newfoundland Museum collection.

236.
A nineteenth century birch spindle back chair employing a naturally shaped piece of wood, similar to a "boat knee", to form each front leg, collected in Placentia Bay. Private collection.

237.
Detail of one of the front legs.

238.
A circa 1900 child's rocking chair with original red paint, collected in Greenspond, Bonavista Bay. Private collection.

239.
A late nineteenth century child's chair, collected in Green's Harbour, Trinity Bay. Private collection.

It appears that, by the late nineteenth century, few chairs of the type normally mass-produced, were made in outport shops. It was most likely more economical for shops, and even local factories, to import them from various Canadian sources, such as, for example, Bass River, Nova Scotia. In fact, according to information gleaned from knowledgeable informants, as well as from material evidence, kitchen and dining room chairs were commonly imported in a "knocked down" condition and assembled at their Newfoundland destinations. Nevertheless, even though such chairs were plentifully available and relatively inexpensive to buy, many outport people chose to make their own homemade versions. The example shown in photo 240 is an example. The squared back spindles, however, can be linked to early twentieth century mission or arts and crafts furniture. Notice that the front legs are carved to suggest they were turned in a lathe.

ENDNOTES

1. See Kinmonth, *Irish Country Furniture, 1700–1950*, 103
2. See Kinmonth, *Irish Country Furniture, 1700–1950*, 10–13
3. *Ibid.*
4. See Cotton's article, "The Research Behind the Exhibition", in *Routes*, 16.

240.
An early twentieth century refinished handmade rocking chair of assorted woods, collected in King's Cove, Bonavista Bay. Private collection.

CHAPTER 13

THE PARLOUR AND DINING ROOM

Unlike the busy informal kitchen, the outport parlour was a formal room and was infrequently used. Because it was reserved for special and formal occasions, such as weddings and funerals, and to entertain important visitors, it normally contained the very best furnishings a family could afford. Items often included high-style and good quality shop and factory-made furniture. And, by the early twentieth century, a fancy imported pump organ became a common item of parlour furniture. Nevertheless, it was not uncommon for these special rooms to contain homemade pieces. And the materials from which some of them were made, clearly reflected conditions of "hard times" (see especially photos 83 and 84 for two examples already discussed).

By the second half of the nineteenth century, the parlour, like the kitchen, usually contained a stove. But, unlike the stove in the kitchen, the one in the parlour was normally highly decorated. The mantel and over mantel of the example shown in photo 241, was made by Henry William Winter of Clarke's Beach. Its original finish is now covered by white paint.

In addition to a stove, parlour furniture almost always included a fancy sideboard on which to display family portraits, nicknacks and souvenirs. The cupboards and drawers of these often elaborate items were mainly used to store a variety of infrequently used objects. The example shown in photo 242 has a number of unusual features. They include applied vertical mouldings enhanced with geometrical incising, on each side of the front of the

243.
Detail of one of the fretted leaf decorations applied to a corner of a door panel.

241.
Parlour stove photographed in Bareneed, Conception Bay during the early 1980s.

242.
A circa 1900 pine sideboard with overhanging top tier, collected in Port Rexton, Trinity Bay. Private collection.

base; a plain flat vertical moulding incised with a herring bone motif, at the centre of the base; fretted leaf decorations applied to the corners of the door panels (photo 243); and applied wooden back plates with scalloped and notched edges, behind the imported pear-shaped pulls on the drawers. Photo 252, incidentally, shows an example of fretwork, similar to that used in the corner of the doors of this sideboard. Most likely, both examples were made by Kenneth Monks, not the maker of this sideboard.

Other ornamentation on the sideboard includes an incised leaf motif outlining the high backboard; incised circular motifs on the apron or plinth; moulded edges around the top of the carcase and the shelf; and fretted gothic inspired decorations (simply begging to be broken off) fixed to the ends of the shelf. Notice that the diamond-like shape of the pendant forming part of the unusually shaped ornament crowning the top of the back-board is similar to that of the finials forming the tops of the protruding shelf supports on the sideboard shown in photo 244. The sideboard is constructed with a combination of round nails, having cross hatch marks on their heads, and square nails. The original rosewood finish has been simulated.

In addition to its depth, an unusual feature of the parlour sideboard shown in photo 244 is the flat, shaped shelf supports which pass completely through the shelf and form finials. The item retains its original dark stain finish under several layers of darkened varnish. The black porcelain knobs are also original.

The example shown in photo 245 has a drawer and cupboard arrangement — one long drawer and a tier of two half width drawers over an enclosed cupboard — which draws its inspiration from mass-produced dining room furniture; the panel separating the two cupboard doors, from outport kitchen dressers; the backboard with its attached shelf, from outport parlour sideboards; and its shallow depth, from Irish vernacular case furniture. The original grained finish of this sideboard — most likely black paint or stain over a brown base — is hidden by a layer of old white paint. Round wire finishing nails are used in the construction. The traditionally shaped tablets on the door and end panels are created with mouldings and applied blocks of wood.

Occasionally, unusually small outport chiffoniers, about the size of washstands having a drawer over an enclosed cupboard, are reported. The example shown in photo 246 is only 107 cm. high, 84 cm. wide, and 44 cm. deep. It has a shelf supported by spindles and backed by scallops. This is a feature which occurs principally around the Cork area of Ireland. Its original door hinges were handmade from thin sheet metal most likely obtained from a metal food container or tin can. Fragments remaining on the doors and the carcass facilitated the making of accurately simulated replacements (photo 247). The original finish is hidden by numerous layers of paint. Another example of an unusually small chiffonier is shown in photo 248. It measures 102 cm. high, 81 cm. wide, and 40 cm. deep and is exceptionally well made. The backboard of this item is enhanced with scalloping and a hand carved whorl, and each end of the drawer front is embellished with two scallops which together resemble the wide end of a heart. While the spotted finish on the drawer front is original, the mahogany finish and wallpapered panels on the

244.
An unusually deep, by outport standards, late nineteenth century pine sideboard collected in Wing's Point, Notre Dame Bay. Private collection.

245.
An unusually shallow late nineteenth century sideboard of assorted woods, collected in the Bonavista Peninsula. Private collection.

247.
Detail of the handmade hinges.

246.
An unusually small nineteenth century chiffonnier of assorted woods, collected in the Placentia Bay area. Private collection.

248.
An unusually small nineteenth century chiffonnier collected in King's Point, Green Bay. Private collection.

remainder of the chiffonnier is a simulation of the original. Construction details include hand cut dovetails in the drawer construction and the use of hand forged nails.

Other parlour furniture, which primarily served to display objects, include whatnots; and even these Victorian icons of mass production were shop-made and homemade in the outports. The pierced decoration of the example shown in photo 249 may have been suggested by the barge board on Hawthorne Cottage, a national historic site located in Brigus.

Fancy shelves and mantlepieces were also handmade for the parlour. The hanging cupboard or shelf shown in photo 250 is an exceptionally skillfully made and pleasingly shaped example. Photo 251 shows a shelf which has metal curtain rod holders attached to the inside surface of each of its supports, indicating it may have been used above a small window or pass-through. It was originally painted, but has been stripped and given a dark red finish.

The pair of fretted brackets shown in photo 252 are puzzling. These items are only eight inches high, and there is much evidence of tedious handwork. For example, the different sections of wood from which each bracket was made are all of different thicknesses, suggesting they were cleft by hand. Furthermore, the elaborately fretted foliage designs were painstakingly cut with a treadle-operated machine. If you could closely examine these brackets, you would see that the leaves and other details which are cut at identical locations in the pattern of each one, differ slightly in both size and outline. Patterns such as the one used for these remarkable brackets were more appropriately employed to decorate wallpaper and textiles. The overall outline of the pattern is in the form of a butterfly, and contained within the butterfly is a smaller outline of a heart. The butterfly, of course, was a popular late nineteenth century motif for embellishing wallpaper and textiles. The fretted sections of the brackets, incidentally, appear to be birch, the shelves, pine.

It is tempting to suspect the shelves were made as love tokens. The relatively sophisticated machinery of the day, in combination with significantly less complicated patterns, allowed swift production of small decorative furnishings at relatively low cost. Under normal circumstances, anyone making time-consuming and difficult-to-make items by hand would most likely not be able to successfully compete with local furniture making shops and mail order catalogues. But the fact is, at least several examples of such intricate fretwork have been found on the Bonavista Peninsula and, in some instances, the fretwork is used merely as a decoration, for example, in the corners of door panels of case pieces (see photo 243). It is the author's opinion that the maker of this fretwork was an individual who did, in fact, specialize in making decorative fretted items, including furniture components, to sell wholesale to local furniture makers and retail to local residents. It is very likely that such an individual was Kenneth Monks who made the remarkable bed shown in photo 120. According to family recollection, when Kenneth Monks was a young man, he seriously injured his back while fishing. The accident resulted from his attempt to haul up a heavy metal anchor into his boat. As a consequence, Monks was no longer

249.
A late nineteenth century pine and birch whatnot enhanced with pierced motifs, collected in Brigus, Conception Bay. Newfoundland Museum collection.

250.
A skillfully made and pleasingly shaped late nineteenth century hanging pine corner cupboard collected in Harbour Grace, Conception Bay. Private collection.

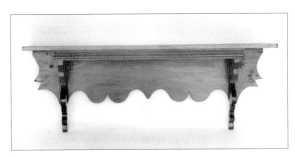

251.
A late nineteenth century pine shelf collected in Bareneed, Conception Bay. Private collection.

252.
A pair of intricately hand-fretted brackets collected in the Bonavista Peninsula, circa 1890. Private collection.

able to do heavy manual work, so he turned to repairing clocks and watches. Considering that he had already been practiced at making fretwork, as evidenced by his bed and his handmade treadle-operated fretwork machine, it is reasonable to suspect that he also began to spend significant amounts of time making small fretted items.

The small wall shelf shown in photo 253 was almost certainly made as a love token. It is entirely hand carved and emulates late nineteenth century, mass-produced wall shelves which were of rectilinear Eastlake form and enhanced with machine carving of a Gothic nature. When collected, the details of the carving were obscured by numerous layers of peeling paint, and the shelf was splintered in numerous places. It has since been restored by Rupert Batten. Incidentally, the small centrally located gothic-shaped aperture most likely originally held a mirror.

The handmade fretted corner shelf shown in photo 254 has a mahogany finish which is a simulation of the original.

The cornice, tapering six sided columns, unyielding straight lines and chaste flat surfaces give the mantlepiece shown in photo 255 a rigid, antiseptic appearance. The severity of the mantle's lines, however, are somewhat mitigated by the decorative bands of garter-like moulding with notched edges, applied around the columns. The maker most likely had access to electrically powered equipment. This would account for the overall precision and neatness of the mantle's construction and the uniformity of the notched work (photo 256). Nevertheless, making the mantle must have demanded considerably skill, especially considering that the six sided columns are tapering. The columns, incidentally, are not hollow, but shaped from solid wood.

Interestingly, the house for which the mantle was made, was built by Mr. Abraham Richards between 1914 and 1918. Mr. Richards initially fished for a living, but later worked at various jobs in St. John's. One was with the United Nail & Foundry Co. Ltd., making moulds and patterns for stoves and for industrial and architectural items. The mantle, however was not made until sometime during the1930s, but not by Mr. Richards. It was

253.
A late nineteenth century hand carved wall shelf made from recycled softwood and collected in the general area of the Avalon Peninsula. Private collection.

254.
A late nineteenth century fretwork decorated corner shelf of pine, collected in Harbour Grace, Conception Bay. Private collection.

255.
A painted pine mantle displaying an unusual synthesis of formal design and folk decoration, collected in Bareneed, Conception Bay. Private collection.

256.
Detail of the notched mouldings applied to the columns.

constructed by Abraham Newell, a local fisherman, chimney builder and carpenter. It is tempting to suspect that Mr. Richards provided Mr. Newell with a pattern from his workplace to make the mantle, considering that its appearance is somewhat reminiscent of a metal or a marble example. Though it is now painted in two contrasting colours, white and medium blue, it appears that the mantle was originally painted entirely in blue.

Round pedestal tables on which tea could be served, were often the largest tables to be found in outport parlours. An example discussed earlier is shown in photo 36. Smaller tables were of many different kinds, and functioned to hold lamps, bibles and other objects. Late nineteenth examples are shown in photos 257, 258, and 259. The example shown in photo 258 retains its original dark mahogany finish; the top was never finished. The sawn flat legs are similar to, and most likely modeled after, flat legs traditionally used on pedestal tables made in the English West Country. It is difficult to know whether the table was made in a local shop or was homemade.

Major forms of parlour seating include upholstered couches (photos 260–263) and sofas. The couches, like the informal kitchen examples, were most often used as a seat to accommodate several people at one time, rather than to semi recline upon.

The general form of the example shown in photo 260 is of high style inspiration, whereas the incised star decoration on the apron and at the top of the legs (photo 261) can be traced to vernacular furniture in southeast Ireland. The original dark mahogany finish has been over painted in white and the couch has been re-upholstered in a plastic material. Residues of fish scales stuck to the material suggest that, in later years, the couch had been relegated to an outbuilding where it had been used as a stand to hold herring.

A portion of the back of the couch shown in photo 262 has been elegantly scrolled to suggest an ocean wave. The couch has been stripped of its upholstery and numerous coats of paint, and stained dark red and varnished to simulate its original finish. The incised

257.
A late nineteenth century lamp table retaining its old dark finish under several subsequently applied coats of varnish, collected in Bonavista, Bonavista Bay. Private collection.

258.
A late nineteenth century lamp table handmade of assorted woods, including birch for the pedestal, collected in Seldom, Fogo Island. Private collection.

259.
A late nineteenth century pine and birch pedestal table collected in Trinity West, Trinity Bay. Private collection.

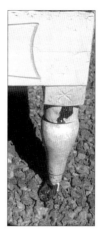

261.
Detail of the incised star on the top of one of the legs.

260.
A nineteenth century pine and birch parlour couch collected in King's Cove, Bonavista Bay. Private collection.

262.
An unusually low nineteenth century pine and birch couch collected in Bonavista, Bonavista Bay. Private collection.

carving on the face of the headrest (photo 264) and on the back of the homemade couch shown in photo 263 is hand done. The small carved detail on the lower end of the back (photo 265) is actually a very functional wedge. It helps to hold the narrow strips of birch in place, which are applied over the outside edge of the scrolled back to give it a more elegant appearance.

Towards the end of the nineteenth century, parlour sets usually consisting of a settee, rocker, armchair and two side chairs became popular items of outport parlour furniture. In addition to being made in St. John's and outport woodworking shops, they were also homemade (see photos 266 and 267).

Needless to say, frames were homemade for use in almost every room of the house.[1] Those made for the parlour to hold photographs and mirrors were often richly embellished with pan-Celtic motifs and/or decorations which can be linked to specific British and Irish regions.

The frame shown in photo 268 is generally of arts and crafts persuasion. The way in which dentils were used to embellish it, however, suggests an additional Irish vernacular influence. Dentils are normally found as a moulding under a cornice on high-style furniture and on buildings. However, they were also used to create decorative edges and borders on vernacular furniture. On outport furniture, they were sometimes used in unusual contexts and in unusual combinations with other related motifs. Notice, for instance, the single scallop in the centre of each band of dentils. Other examples having unusual combinations of edge decorations include the frame shown in photo 269 and the chest of drawers shown in photo 337. The frame retains its original black finish.

The cross-corner frame shown in photo 269 and 270 combines dentil decoration with various other motifs. These include scallops scooped from the forward front edge of the frame, and sawteeth. Each dentil is formed in the centre of a scooped scallop, and

264.
Detail of the carving on the back and on the face of the headrest.

263.
A late nineteenth century pine and birch couch homemade by Joseph Batten in Bareneed, Conception Bay. Private collection.

265.
Detail of the decorative wedge.

266.
A rocking chair from an early twentieth century parlour set made of assorted woods by Henry William Winter in Clarke's Beach, Conception Bay. Private collection.

267.
A rather exuberant looking circa 1900 settee made as part of a larger set, collected in Bonavista, Bonavista Bay. Private collection.

269.
A late nineteenth century cross-corner pine frame enhanced with applied hand carved birch leaves at the corners and displaying an unusual use of dentil decoration in combination with other motifs, collected in Conception Bay North.

268.
An early twentieth century pine cross-corner frame made to hold four images, collected in the Bonavista Peninsula. Private collection.

270.
Detail of photo 269.

a sawtooth is formed where the ends of each scallop meet (see photos 206 and 311 for examples of items decorated with more orthodox sawtooth and scalloped borders). The simple incised carving of relatively straight lines on the inside edge of the frame, incidentally, is most likely a form of rope twist carving. The maker of this ingeniously designed frame is almost certainly the same person who made the comb box shown in photo 196, the frame in photo 271 and the chest of drawers shown in photo 337.

The current owner of the frame shown in photo 271 naively believed it was made significantly out of square. Nevertheless, because of the novel way in which it was decorated, he used it to hold a print. However, he oriented the frame and the print in a horizontal position. When the frame is turned vertically (photo 272) it no longer appears out of square.

Photo 273 shows an outport cross corner frame enhanced with rope twist carving. Such carving began to be used extensively in the early nineteenth century following its rising popularity owing to Nelson's successful naval battles. Though it was normally used as a moulding on high-style furniture throughout Britain, it was also commonly used to embellish vernacular furniture in Southern Ireland. This practice, as was mentioned earlier, was introduced to Newfoundland by the early Irish settlers. It is interesting that, during the late nineteenth and early twentieth century, cross-corner frames, enhanced with rope twist carving, were frequently to be found in Roman Catholic homes in Southern Ireland, as well as in the outports of Newfoundland. In Ireland, they were used to hold various religious images. Since cross corner frames were not made until around 1870, the mutual tradition suggests that aspects of traditional furniture making in the outports and in Ireland continued along similar paths long after migration to Newfoundland and Labrador had ceased. (see photos 46 and 49 for an example of a matching outport dresser and washstand enhanced with rope twist carving).

Another outport frame of Irish vernacular inspiration is shown in photo 274. It is decorated with hand carved fans and chip carving. Fan or shell carvings were often used in Britain generally to enhance the inside corners of doors, drawers and panels of high-style

271.
A circa 1900 pine cross-corner frame intended to be hung vertically with the wide end at the bottom and the top end tilting forward, collected in Conception Bay North. Private collection.

272.
The frame in photo 271 shown in a vertical position.

273.
A circa 1900 pine cross-corner frame enhanced with rope twist carving, collected in Conception Bay North Shore. Private collection.

274.
A nineteenth century frame of strong Irish character, made from recycled mahogany and decorated with applied fan carvings and a band of chip carving resembling sawteeth, collected in Carbonear, Conception Bay. Private collection.

furniture. They were also commonly used by Irish carpenters to embellish items of Irish Country furniture (see photo 77). Chip carving was often used in Ireland in combination with various other motifs. It was likely introduced to Ireland from Scandinavia.

The frame shown in photo 275 is embellished with unusually small fan motifs, in relation to the size of the frame and the applied corner blocks carved with birch leaves. The carving on the frame shown in photo 276 has a strong Irish "feel", but the potted tulip motif on the corners suggests an additional European influence.

Photo 277 shows a frame enhanced with an innovative version of applied leaves at the corners. Several grouped together form the outline of a flying wheel, a motif commonly used as a decoration in the Celtic areas of Britain, including Ireland, Scotland, Wales, the Channel Islands and Cornwall in England. This motif, in combination with bands of diamonds and the gouge-carved decoration, gives the frame an Irish, or perhaps Welsh, character.

Some of the original hearts are missing from the frame shown in photo 278, and have been replaced. The original ones were created by layering wood, much in the way tramp art was made. In this case, however, the layers were very thin, and their edges were joined together and carved to create a single rounded edge. The heart motif, incidentally, was commonly used in both Ireland and Wales as a love token.

Applied hearts also enhance the corners of the frame made by John Mugford and shown in photo 279, while diamonds are carved in relief on its surface. Other carving on the frame only vaguely resembles the bark which is simulated on mass-produced examples. Notice the "V"-shaped incising inside the hearts (photo 280). It is similar to that on the hearts decorating Mugford's profusely carved washstand (photo 73).

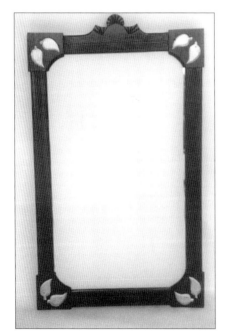

275.
An early twentieth century pine mirror frame perhaps displaying a combination of Art Deco and Irish vernacular influences, collected in Bay Roberts, Conception Bay. Private collection.

276.
A late nineteenth century cross-corner pine frame, collected in Conception Bay North Shore. Private collection.

277.
A late nineteenth century pine cross-corner frame collected in Port de Grave, Conception Bay. Private collection.

278.
A large early twentieth century frame generously embellished with applied hearts and retaining its original red finish with gold highlights, collected in Port de Grave, Conception Bay.

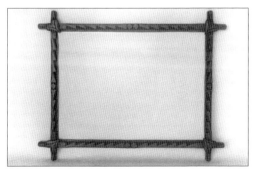

279.
An early twentieth century refinished cross-corner pine frame enhanced with pan-Celtic motifs, reputed to have been made by Mr. John Mugford of Port de Grave. Private collection.

280.
Closeup of the left hand side of the frame.

Photo 281 shows a frame embellished with sawteeth. See photo 312 for a wash-stand which also is enhanced with this form of decoration. It was collected in the same general area.

Carving resembling the teeth of a saw was not the only construction related shapes employed to decorate outport frames. A frame enhanced with a nail head motif is shown in photo 282, while a frame decorated with hobnail carving is shown in photo 283.

The inspiration for hobnail carving can be traced to Southern Ireland. Hobnails were nails having raised heads, two rows of which were put around the rim of the soles of boots. The hobnail motif is also similar to patterns used to decorate cut glass, and Waterford and Cork were early glass-making areas. On Irish vernacular furniture, this motif was normally limited to panels and relatively small areas. On the frame shown in photo 283, however, it covers the entire surface. The hobnail pattern was traditionally created by using saws, chisels, knives and even files. In this instances, the choice of tool was most likely a saw. See photo 114 for an outport washstand decorated with several different versions of hobnail carving.

The notched corner decorations on the frame shown in photo 284 suggest corner holders used in photograph albums; the gold-painted tree motif on the elongated lozenges is probably employed as a fertility symbol. It consists of two coniferous trees, one a mirror reflection of the other, in a vertically oriented alignment and two stubby deciduous trees or bushes in a horizontal alignment, their trunks connected at the centre of the lozenge. This motif, together with the applied hearts and "corner holders" suggest the item was made as a wedding gift to hold a wedding photograph. For other examples of outport furniture enhanced with a tree motif, see photos 37, 307 and 319.

Unlike the frame shown in photo 284, the cross-corner frame shown in photo 285 is very plain. The carvings of oak leaves applied to its corners, however, are enhanced with

281.
An early twentieth century pine frame embellished with sawteeth, collected near Bonavista, Bonavista Bay. Private collection.

282.
A circa 1900 pine frame enhanced with a nailhead motif, collected in Port de Grave, Conception Bay. Private collection.

283.
A mid nineteenth century pine frame decorated with hobnail carving and bands of contrasting colours, collected in Carbonear, Conception Bay. Private collection.

284.
A late nineteenth century frame retaining its original black finish with gold highlights, and decorated with applied carving reminiscent of tramp-art, collect in Harbour Grace, Conception Bay. Private collection.

285.
A very plain late nineteenth century cross-corner frame having oak leaves enhanced with diaper carving, on each corner (photo 286). Private collection.

286.
Detail of the diaper carving on one of the leaves. Oak trees, incidentally, are not native to Newfoundland and Labrador.

diaper carving (photo 286). A more dramatic example of diaper carving can be seen on the pipe box shown in photo 287. The box is carved from a single piece of wood.

Diaper carving was used to enhance country furniture in southern Ireland. The inspiration for this embellishment can be traced to the fifteenth century in Ypres in Flanders where there was a major settlement of Irish nuns. Diaper was a form of decoration impressed into linen and hence the association with very shallow cutting or incising.

Some, but not all, outport houses contained a dining room. Furniture used in this room included imported and locally made dining and serving tables, buffets, sideboards, display cabinets and chairs. The large pedestal table shown in photo 288 was made by Henry William Winter. It is constructed with round wire nails and has been refinished. The older shop-made table shown in photo 289 has drop leaves on its ends, rather than on its sides where they are more normally found. Each leaf is supported by a slim wooden rail which pivots at its centre from a slot cut in the apron. The original dark mahogany finish of this table has been simulated.

The dining room sideboard shown in photo 290 was also most likely shop-made. Notice the unusually wide recycled boards forming the back of the carcase (photo 291). The one shown in photo 292, however, though it was very skillfully crafted, is an example of a homemade dining room sideboard. The applied carvings and the ionic capitals were shaped using hand tools. The item is made mostly of pine. However, there is some use of early plywood.

Two early dining chairs of possible Scottish regional inspiration are shown in photo 293. The chair on the left has a birch seat inset into the apron; the chair on the right has a padded seat. Both have been refinished. Brass rather than wooden pins were used to secure the mortice and tenon joints in the seat frames of both examples. These chairs, as well as the

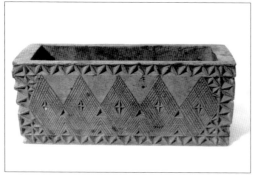

287.
A nineteenth century diaper carved birch pipe box, collected in Upper Gullies, Conception Bay. Private collection.

288.
A large early twentieth century pine and birch pedestal table made by Henry William Winter in Clarke's Beach, Conception Bay. Private collection.

289.
A nineteenth century pine and birch dining table having a drop leaf on each of its two ends, collected in the North Shore, Conception Bay. Private collection.

290.
A circa 1900 pine dining room sideboard retaining its original oak grained finish, made in the resettled community of Ireland's Eye, Trinity Bay. Private collection.

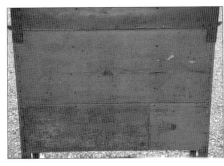

291.
Detail of the wide boards forming the back of the carcase.

292.
A homemade dining room sideboard by Joseph Batten in Bareneed, Conception Bay. Newfoundland Museum collection.

two shown in photo 294, were most likely made for and used in the dining room of a local merchant. In this photo, the chair on the right is one of a set of six collected in Hibb's Cove, Conception Bay; the one on the left was collected in nearby Cupids. The back of the armchair and the curved apron are generously reeded. The crest rail is a single piece of wood (photo 295). Both chairs have been stripped of numerous coats of paint. They were most likely made by the same craftsman.

Photo 296 shows one of a set of two kitchen or dining room chairs made in the early twentieth century. Its back was modeled after a mass-produced dining room chair of the day. A single naturally-shaped piece of wood or "boat knee" was used to form each front leg. This chair, as well as the one shown in photo 297, was possibly homemade. That particular chair is also one of a pair. It is constructed of assorted woods, including oak. The strapwork decoration on the crest rail (photo 298) was incised using a simple hand tool. The chair shown in photo 299 was almost certainly made in a local shop. It is one of a set of three which were made of assorted woods. The hand carved crest and intermediate rail, for example, are oak. The chair has been stripped of its many coats of paint, and the seat covering was missing when the chair was collected. What especially suggests the chair was shop-made is the way the side aprons are joined to the front legs using screws.

293.
Two circa 1840 birch and maple side chairs, possibly of Scottish regional inspiration, collected in Port de Grave, Conception Bay. Private collection.

294.
Two birch chairs with pine seats, of possible Scottish regional inspiration. Side chair: Newfoundland Museum collection; armchair. Private collection.

295.
Detail of the back of the armchair.

296.
One of a set of two early twentieth century painted kitchen or dining room chairs made of assorted woods and collected in Garnish, Fortune Bay. Newfoundland Museum collection.

297.
One of a pair of early twentieth century dining chairs with padded seats, collected in Herring Neck, Notre Dame Bay. Private collection.

298.
Strapwork decoration on the crest rail of the chair in photo 297.

299.
One of a set of three relatively low-seated nineteenth century chairs collected in Colliers, Conception Bay. Private collection.

Upholstered couches were also sometimes added to the furniture of outport dining rooms. Many of the very early and finely made surviving examples of outport dining room furniture were made originally for the more spacious residences of merchants and other well-to-do outport people.

ENDNOTE

1. See Dr. Gerald L. Pocius' article, "Holy Pictures In Newfoundland Houses: Visual Codes For Secular And Supernatural Relationships", in *Laurentian University Review*, Vol. X11, No. 1 (November 1979), 101–125, for a detailed discussion concerning how the walls of Newfoundland dwellings are used as vehicles of display.

CHAPTER 14

THE BEDROOM

Perhaps because many bedrooms lacked a fireplace or a stove, they were used for little more than retiring for the night, washing oneself and attending to private and hygienic needs. Important items of bedroom furniture usually consisted only of a bed, a washstand or a related piece, a blanket box and/or one or several chests of drawers.

Stump beds were commonly used throughout the rural areas of Britain until the nineteenth century. This type of bed was most likely the earliest to have been made in the outports. Photo 300 shows a partly original and partly reproduced example. Three of its four painted birch legs are all that survive of an early nineteenth century outport bed, and are the only evidence that stump beds were made in the outports. The high post bed shown in photo 301, however is virtually complete. It is shown in the Newfoundland Museum's workshop being assembled for repairs. It retains its original red ochre stain. Examples of this type of bed are now difficult to find in the outports. More commonly found are adult size beds similar to the on shown in photo 302. This rare child's bed now forms part of the furnishings of the Cape Bonavista Lighthouse, a provincial historic site. It retains several layers of old darkened varnish over a mahogany stain. The miniature sideboard beside the bed was also collected in Bonavista. The doll's bed, or cradle shown in photo 303 is generally similar to locally-made hooded cradles, except for the end which is carved to suggest a heart.

300.
A partly original and partly reproduced early nineteenth century stump bed assembled for display in the Newfoundland Museum's exhibit, Routes: Exploring the British Origins of Newfoundland Outport Furniture Design.

301.
A mid nineteenth century pine and birch high post bed, collected in Port Rexton, Trinity Bay. Newfoundland Museum collection.

An enormous variety of washstands were made in the outports. Notice that the towel rail supports of the shop-made washstand shown in photo 304 and the mirror supports on the matching bureau (photo 305) are shaped to suggest lighted candles. The washstand shown in photo 306 was homemade. Notice that part of the shape of the bottom edge of the front and side aprons (seen more clearly on the side apron), is an adaptation of the heart motif enhancing the settle which was photographed in the same house (photo 211). On the settle, the shape resembling the wide end of a heart is cut from both the top edge of the back and the bottom edge of the apron. The shape of a complete heart is also carved into the back of a couch (photo 221) used in the same kitchen.

The highly decorated and unusual washstand shown in photo 307 was homemade, and is of a style localised in the South East of Ireland. The original finish is hidden by many coats of paint, but has been simulated over the top layer. However, the painted tree motif used here as a fertility symbol, is the original. The scooped disks on the front, incidentally, were most likely formed with a pot auger, and what appears to be a door below the drawer is actually a hatch or cover; it is not hinged. This particular washstand was probably made as a love token.

The pierced shape centered low in the backboard of the washstand shown in photo 308 has been closed off by a thin slab of wood, perhaps when the washstand was first made. Round wire finishing nails were used in the construction and the original rosewood finish has been simulated. The towel rails and their front supports are replacements. Notice that the elaborately moulded simulated panels on the ends of the washstand and surrounding the drawer front are somewhat similar to those on the apron of the much older stand shown in photo 205.

302.
A mid nineteenth century pine and birch bed made for a child and collected in Bonavista, Bonavista Bay. Newfoundland Museum collection.

303.
A late nineteenth century pine doll's cradle retaining its original light grey painted finish, collected in Greenspond, Bonavista Bay. Private collection.

304.

A late nineteenth century painted washstand photographed in the bedroom of a house in Pools Island, Bonavista Bay, during the late 1970s.

305.

The matching bureau for the washstand shown in photo 304.

306.

A circa 1900 painted pine and birch washstand photographed in the house for which it was made in Hibb's Cove, Port de Grave.

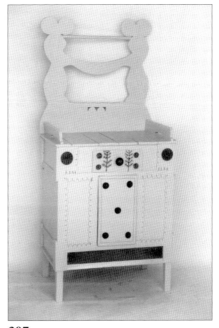

307.

A late nineteenth century washstand of assorted softwoods, collected in Bonavista, Bonavista Bay. Private collection.

Photo 309 shows a washstand having a combination of British regional and English high-style embellishments. For example, the gothic arches carved in relief on the door front and applied on the sides, were inspired by the mid nineteenth century gothic revival style. Motifs similar to the carved star surrounding a sculptured disk, as seen on the back-board and on the drawer front, were frequently used to decorate country furniture in Celtic regions such as Ireland, Scotland, Wales, Cornwall in England, and the Channel Islands. The notching on the edges of the drawer fronts, however, can be linked to English West Country tradition. In that particular region, the edges of spinning wheel beds and small benches were similarly embellished (see photo 310). In addition to being decorative, such notching helped to protect the vulnerable end grain.

The design of the washstand shown in photo 311 is somewhat puzzling. Except for the two white porcelain knobs which are centred on one of the four aprons to create an illusion of drawers, and the applied band of scalloping, it would not be possible to tell what side constituted the front of this particular washstand. The aprons on all four sides are similarly scalloped and the towel rails are held both at the front and at the back by similarly shaped supports. Normally, the backs of towel rails used on this type of washstand were fixed to or socketed into a backboard, not into supports similar to those used on the front.

Creating the illusion of drawers, incidentally, was commonly practiced by Irish vernacular furniture makers.[1] Because wood was scarce and making drawers required a significant amount of it, they were considered a luxury. Consequently, it was impressive to have them, so they were often faked.

Scalloping was traditionally used as a form of decoration by Irish carpenters and joiners. It was an easy way to embellish the edges of common furniture when only simple hand tools were at one's disposal. The form of scalloping employed on this particular wash-stand — segments of circles — is frequently found on outport furniture. Another related form of border decoration often found, is comprised of a series of projections with pointed ends, referred to as "sawteeth". An example can be seen in photo 312. These two different versions of decorative borders can be seen employed together on the wall shelf of Irish inspiration shown in photo 199 and the bedroom dressing stand, photo 341. A chip carved version of sawteeth can be seen in photos 186 and 344.

An obvious high-style influence on the design of this vernacular washstand can be seen in the square tapering legs of late eighteenth century origin. Forged nails are used in the construction, and the original black painted finish has been simulated.

Like the example just discussed, the washstand shown in photo 312 is also of Irish vernacular flavour, it pretends to have a drawer and its original black finish has been simulated. Notice the band of sawteeth is applied to the front of the top of the washstand with their pointed ends standing proud. Presumably, this was to help prevent items from falling over the edge. The applied rectangles with their edges enhanced with sawteeth is also an interesting feature (photo 313). A major portion of the backboard, one of the towel rails and the front towel rail supports have been restored by Michael Smith. Photo 314 shows the washstand as it looked before its restoration. As can be clearly seen, the earlier

308.
A late nineteenth century pine and birch washstand collected in the north shore of Trinity Bay. Private collection.

309.
A late nineteenth century washstand enhanced with Gothic, pan-Celtic and English West Country embellishments, collected in Clarke's Beach, Conception Bay. Private collection.

310.
Detail of the end of a large outport walking wheel which is enhanced with notching similar to that found on English West Country examples. Newfoundland Museum collection.

311.
A nineteenth century pine and birch washstand of Irish vernacular inspiration, collected in Bonavista, Bonavista Bay.

repairs are naively executed and employ a poorer grade of wood than the original. Though numerous outport people were, in fact, naturally skilled, not everyone was so blessed.

A washstand of entirely different design is shown in photo 315. Boldly shaped pieces are applied to the opening between the upper and lower shelves at the front of the washstand perhaps to help conceal what was kept on the lower shelf. Though, normally what was put there would cause few even extremely sensitive individuals to blush: a large ewer to hold water for washing oneself. Interestingly, this unusual decorative addition would necessitate placing and retrieving the ewer through one of the side openings, rather than directly through the front. Many layers of paint have been carefully dry scraped from the washstand to uncover the original coat of grey paint. Forged nails are used in the construction.

Interesting features of the washstand shown in photo 316 include the unusual open gallery and the hand carved legs. The original towel rails which formed part of the gallery were missing when the item was collected and have been replaced. The white paint is either the original coat or is an old overcoat.

The washstand shown in photo 317 is ingeniously designed. Each of its four legs is naturally-shaped and has a top end which curves outwards to form a towel rail support.

Photo 318 shows a washstand which is very similar to an example collected by the Canadian Museum of Civilization, Culture Studies Division during the 1970s, and shown on page 178 of *The Traditional Furniture of Outport Newfoundland*, Harry Cuff Publications Limited, St. John's, 1983. What appears to be a door is not. It is merely a plywood or laminated wood cover and is not fitted with any kind of hardware. Both square and round nails are used in the construction. The author has encountered at least one other outport washstand having a cupboard fitted with a cover, rather than a door (see photo 307). Similarly functioning covers have also been found on an outport kitchen dresser (photo 173).

312.
A nineteenth century pine and birch washstand of Irish inspiration, collected in Bonavista, Bonavista Bay. Private collection.

313.
Detail of sawteeth decoration.

314.
The washstand shown in photo 312 before its most recent repairs and restoration.

315.
A nineteenth century pine and birch washstand of unusual design, collected in Bonavista, Bonavista Bay. Private collection.

316.
A late nineteenth century pine and birch washstand of Irish vernacular persuasion, collected in Open Hall, Bonavista Bay. Private collection.

317.
An ingeniously designed nineteenth century painted washstand of assorted woods, collected in Conception Bay North Shore. Private collection.

When collected, the original finish of the very impressive washstand shown in photo 319 had been over painted in white. Most of this old overcoat, however, has been removed to reveal its original white and contrasting brown colours. The numerous embellishments range from a large carved stylized birch tree applied on each end, to the relatively small incised and painted motif on the apron of the shelf (photo 320) and the fish tail motif centred on the front and end aprons. Fretwork decorated areas include the drawer front, the applied band of wood above it, and the fronts of the sloped boxes attached to the backboard and flanking the shelf. The turned posts forming each leg and the frame of the washstand is also a highly unusual detail to see on an outport case piece. Curious, as well, is the way the door panels are covered by a patterned material and held in place behind glass , a feature somewhat reminiscent of high-style Regency sideboard doors. Because there is a division between the two doors, incidentally, there is not sufficient room to easily maneuver even a small chamber pot or other relatively large object into the cupboard. Presumably, the washstand was made as a wedding gift. The impressive tree motif most likely represents the hope for fertility and the continuity of family line.

The items shown in photos 321 and 322 were made to perform only some of the functions of a washstand. Photo 321 shows an unusual late nineteenth century combination chest of drawers and dressing table. It is made of pine and retains its original crackled finish. Photo 322 shows a chest having one drawer and a cupboard enclosed by a door. The cupboard was most likely used to store a chamber pot. The item still has its original finish intact.

318.
A circa 1900 painted and carved pine washstand collected in Lower Island Cove, Conception Bay. Private collection.

319.
A late nineteenth century pine washstand of highly unusual design, collected in Dover, Bonavista Bay, but reputed to have been made in Silver Fox Island. Private collection.

320.
Detail of the incised and painted design on the apron of the shelf.

321.
An unusual late nineteenth century combination chest of drawers and dressing table made of pine and retaining its original finish, collected in Victoria Cove, Gander Bay. Private collection.

322.
A nineteenth century chest having one drawer and a cupboard enclosed by a door, collected in Port de Grave, Conception Bay. Private collection.

Blanket boxes were used to store items of clothing. Those having handles to make them more easily portable for travelling, were also used in the bedroom when they were not needed for sea voyages.

The blanket box shown in photo 323 has an unusually enhanced lid or cover. It has been partly opened to better show its deep and heavily moulded frieze. The plinth is scalloped on the back, as well as the front. The box is lap jointed, and forged nails are used in the construction. Photo 324 shows a panelled example.

Painting a vessel on the underside of a travelling box cover (photo 326) was a common nineteenth century practice in both Britain and North America. It was also done in the outports, but relatively few examples have been found. The box shown in photo 325 is sloped on all four sides to provide stability on a moving vessel, and is of dovetailed construction. In the outports, travelling boxes were used to hold clothing and other personal belongings for seasonal voyages to the coast of Labrador for fishing, and for seal hunting. Small items such as shaving gear and writing materials were kept in a lidded till at one end. As was mentioned above, when not being used for this purpose, travelling boxes were often employed in the bedroom for storing blankets and items of clothing. Some eventually were permanently removed to the work shop and used as tool and storage boxes. The travelling box shown in photo 327 is a relatively ordinary example which was made more interesting by the addition of chip carving on the beckets (photo 328).

Like blanket boxes, chests of drawers were commonly made in the outports. The example shown in photo 329 was photographed in an antiques shop in Bay Roberts, Conception Bay. It has been recently repainted. The example shown in photo 330, however retains its original grained rosewood finish. Its most important feature is the applied blocks of hob nail carving (photo 331) flanking the top drawer. Hob nail carving links this example to Southern Ireland (see photos 114 and 283). Nails with rectangular heads are used in the construction; the wooden knobs are replacements. The chest of drawers

323.
A nineteenth century refinished pine blanket box collected in Open Hall, Bonavista Bay. Bay. Private collection.

324.
A nineteenth century panelled pine blanket box collected in Conception Bay North Shore. Private collection.

325.

A nineteenth century pine travelling box having a ship's painting on the inside of the hinged lid (photo 321), collected in Conception Bay North Shore. Private collection.

327.

A nineteenth century pine painted travelling box, collected in Conception Bay North Shore. Private collection.

326.

The painting on the underside of the cover.

328.
Detail of the chip carved beckets.

329.
A nineteenth century pine chest of drawers collected in the Bonavista Peninsula. Private collection.

shown in photo 332 also has features which can be traced to Ireland. Its shallowness and scalloped apron suggest an Irish vernacular influence. The chest retains its original coat of red paint. The top, however, was never painted. The white porcelain knobs are most likely the original.

Like many vernacular Irish examples, the outport chest of drawers shown in photo 333 has a few eccentric characteristics. For example, not all of the shaped blocks are carved; those on the front of the chest have been left unfinished. Another off-beat detail is the single drawer pulls centred in the long drawers. Embellishments such as the simple carved decoration applied around the top (photo 334), and the recessed decoration on the drawer fronts, were used extensively in Ireland, but were similarly used elsewhere. Like much Irish vernacular case furniture, however, this item is relatively shallow.

Photo 335 shows a bedroom dresser which combines various elements of dresser design not normally seen together. Furthermore, the surface of the mirror frame is unusually sculptured and enhanced with a simple incised design (photo 336).

The remarkable chest of drawers shown in photo 337 deserves special attention. This cleverly designed and innovative item is profusely decorated with motifs which can be traced to South East Ireland. The individual details are very strong, particularly the sculptured hearts, dentils and the shell or fan carvings, a motif often used by Irish carpenters especially to enhance the inside corners of panels and drawers (see photo 338). The positioning of the dentils which are carved in relief on the drawer fronts, as well as the way they were formed, is most unusual. Normally, dentils — a serious of equally spaced rectangular blocks — are used to enhance horizontal cornices. Also unusual is the detail of the single sawtooth centred in each vertical row of dentils. Normally sawteeth are employed to create decorative borders and edges (see, for example, 312 and 281). Here, like the dentils, they are carved on the forward edge of the wood, rather than completely through it. Interestingly, the frame shown in photo 269 is enhanced with similarly carved sawteeth, and,

330.
A nineteenth century pine chest of drawers retaining its original rosewood painted finish, collected in Conception Bay North Shore. Private collection.

331.
Detail of the hob nail carving.

332.
An unusually shallow mid nineteenth century pine chest of drawers with birch top, collected in Champneys East, Trinity Bay. Canadian Museum of Civilization, Culture Studies Division collection.

333.
A late nineteenth century pine chest of drawers retaining its original red-painted finish, collected in Keels, Bonavista Bay. Private collection.

334.
Detail of the applied decorations.

335.
A circa 1900 white painted bedroom dresser collected in Green's Harbour, Trinity Bay. Private collection.

336.
Detail of the sculptured mirror frame.

they are also employed in an innovative way with other related motifs. The chest of drawers and the frame were almost certainly made by the same individual. Incidentally, the outline of the bottom edge of each end apron includes two stylized sawteeth which are formed in a more orthodox manner (photo 339). They are cut completely through the edge of the apron. Sawteeth in chip carved form are also used to create the six pointed star motif on the legs (photo 340). When collected, the original top of the carcase was missing. It has been replaced by a simulated marble one. There is no evidence of a fixed wooden one having been there. Perhaps the original was, in fact, marble. Several late nineteenth century outport case pieces having marble tops have been found in the same general area. Another possibility is that this item was the bottom half of a chest on chest. But there is no evidence to support this either.

Like much Irish country furniture, the dressing stand shown in photo 341 is unusually shallow. Furthermore, particularly the detail of the heart-shaped feet (photo 342) and the applied band of alternating scallops and sawteeth, give the stand a decidedly Irish "feel". Another interesting feature is the shaped mirror supports which somewhat resemble horses' hames.

The decorative band of scallops and sawteeth, incidentally, was most likely put there to hide a mistake. Just out of sight and flanking the mirror supports behind it are two slots cut completely through the top of the dresser (photo 343). They were originally made to hold the bottom ends of the supports. Presumably, a sufficiently large piece of mirror glass could not be obtained to do what was originally planned, and so the supports had to be moved closer together.

While numerous relatively large containers such as blanket boxes and chest of drawers were used in the outports to store items of clothing, few small containers made specifically to store items such as hats have been reported. The chip carved hat box shown in

337.
A late nineteenth century chest of drawers made from assorted woods, including end panels made from early plywood, and collected in Conception Bay North Shore. Private collection.

338.
Detail of drawer fronts.

339.
Detail of the sawteeth on one of the side aprons.

340.
Detail of carved decoration on the feet.

341.
An early twentieth century refinished dressing stand of assorted woods, collected in Fogo Island. Private collection.

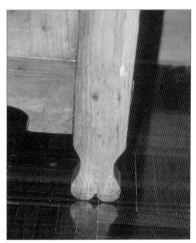

342.
Detail of heart-shaped feet.

343.
Detail of slots cut through the top of the dresser.

photo 344 is an especially rare example. A very old grey paint was removed from a portion of its cover to show the original black finish. The chip carving on the cover, incidentally, is similar to that on the kitchen wall hanging box shown in photo 186. The chip carving on the hand sewn fingers is of a different pattern and create the illusion of cane. Photo 345 shows the stitching visible on the box's interior.

In addition to the many items discussed above, bedroom furniture usually included a small table and a chair or two. Often chairs were made, or existing ones converted, to serve as potties. The example shown in photo 346 reflects an Irish/British Isles tradition, but has a decidedly Irish character. Few potties were as pleasingly shaped as the one shown in photo 347. The example shown in photo 348 is, of course, an example of a chair which at some time in its history, was crudely converted into a potty. Except for each front leg and side apron, which was made from naturally shaped birch, the chair is most likely of Scottish regional inspiration. It retains its original finish of blue paint. Notice the exaggerated rake of the back.

Photo 349 shows a homemade potty chair of special interest. Its general form and decoration might suggest to some that it is a circa 1900 mass-produced "pressed-back" chair which has been converted. Unlike pressed patterns, however, those enhancing the back rails of this particular chair were not made by steaming the wood and mechanically pressing them onto the surface. Pressed patterns show no end grain on their edges. The edges of those on this chair do. And that is because they are actually cut or incised into the surface of the wood using a hand tool (photo 350).

More than one model was used to make this chair. The hand shaped arms, for example, are a type typically found on factory-made Boston rockers. The arms on circa 1900 pressed-back chairs are usually flat. Yet another model was used for the hand carved and squared, rather than rounded, front legs and spindles supporting the arms. In most

344.
A hat box enhanced with chip carving, collected in Bonavista, Bonavista Bay, circa 1840. Private collection.

345.
Detail of the hand stitching on the interior of the hat box.

346.
A late nineteenth century child's potty chair made from assorted woods and collected in the general area of Green's Harbour, Trinity Bay. Private collection.

347.
A nineteenth century pine potty chair enhanced with coach or carriage style painting, collected in Topsail, Conception Bay, but it may have been made in Harbour Grace, Conception Bay. Private collection.

348.
A mid nineteenth century birch chair with pine seat, collected in Port Rexton, Trinity Bay. Newfoundland Museum collection.

349.
An early twentieth century homemade potty chair of birch and oak, collected in Bonavista, Bonavista Bay. Private collection.

350.
Detail of cut decorations on chair back.

cases, when outport furniture makers had no access to a lathe, spindles and legs were shaped in rounded form by hand to simulate lathe work. In fact, the six spindles in the back of this homemade chair, as well as one of the two spindles supporting each arm, were formed in this manner. The design of the chair also deviates from that of conventional pressed-back models in that the stiles forming the back are squared rather than rounded. And, furthermore, the stiles, unlike those of Windsor type chairs, continue below the seat to form the back legs. By tastefully combining a variety of normally unrelated design elements, the chair's maker has created a unique and innovative item. The hatch-like seat cover, incidentally, which is now visibly warped, simply lifts off the seat, and a hinged flap at the rear allows access to the enclosed storage area underneath the seat.

ENDNOTE

1.   See Kinmonth, *Irish Country Furniture, 1700–1950*, 142–149.

CHAPTER 15

CONCLUSION

After reviewing this book, some readers might suspect that many of the items selected for discussion are one-of-a-kind, bizarre creations, not typical examples of outport furniture. They will be partly correct. Many of the pieces are, in fact, unique. But, they are, nevertheless, typical of outport furniture. Outport people, whether they be highly skilled wood workers or simply handy individuals, have always enjoyed making things with their hands; and making unique and innovative furniture was a common practice until relatively recent years. Furthermore, in addition to crafting basically utilitarian items, skilled outport furniture makers routinely made "special" furniture either for themselves or for their customers; and handy people (as well as those not so handy) made objects as love tokens, or to acknowledge special people or events. Few outport people, however, would consider their creations to be bizarre. Their furniture designs were not vaguely conceived as in a dream, nor did they mysteriously materialize from the ether. Virtually all the pieces shown in this book were crafted following models which were, in most cases, familiar to people living in the communities in which they were made. Furthermore, the local practice of adapting and combining unrelated elements of design from several different models to make a single item was not due to ignorance or naivety. This strategy was commonly pursued by high-style furniture designers. Even the famous Thomas Chippendale did it. In fact, many examples of outport "aberrant" design which resulted from this practice have no less merit than many of his vaunted examples. The main difference is that outport designs did not have the advantage of being popularized through publication as Chippendale's had. Needless to say, the many virtues of outport furniture outline above are the author's personal opinion. Outport furniture is most likely not viewed in such a positive light by the vast majority of collectors of Canadian antique furniture.

There is growing interest in outport furniture in the Canadian antiques market. But, it appears that, in this domain, outport furniture is not entirely understood. Some dealers and collectors refer to the more plain looking and less skillfully made outport items as "primitives" while others label the pieces which are richly endowed with important cultural signatures and information as "folky". In fact, much outport furniture offered in the Canadian market place is not even advertised as such. Antiques pickers and dealers, especially from the province of Quebec, have been regularly visiting Newfoundland for decades and carrying away truck loads of outport furniture for the mainland market. There is evidence that much of this furniture is being passed off as either Maritime or Quebec pieces. Masquerading outport pieces as Early Quebec furniture, in fact, is not difficult to do, especially if it involves the more highly decorated items. Outport furniture, like early Quebec and some Maritime furniture, was often embellished with hearts, diamonds, compass roses and flying wheels, motifs introduced by settlers from various European countries such as France and Germany and the Celtic regions in Britain. Furthermore, because of the realities of settlement in Quebec, Irish vernacular design has stamped its distinctive mark on Quebec furniture just as it has on the outport product. Consequently, the design and decoration of some outport items — or elements of it — are closely similar to those of some Quebec pieces.

To be fair, while Canadians generally, know exceedingly little about outport furniture, the people of Newfoundland and Labrador, are equally uninformed. Ignorance surrounding the subject of country furniture in general appears to be the status quo for the vast majority of North Americans. For the most part, it seems that North American furniture enthusiasts are interested in country furniture primarily for its nostalgic appeal and its ability to create an informal decor. These words are spoken, not to point the finger of blame, but to heighten awareness of the need to address a sorry situation.

Originally, the author had intended to place more emphasis in this book on furniture design transmission from Britain to Newfoundland, and to provide more photographs of British analogues for the outport pieces discussed in it. Such a task, even as little as twenty years ago, would have been next to impossible to accomplish. At that time, furniture history research in Britain focused almost exclusively on formal high-style furniture, the furniture produced for the privileged few. The relatively recent interest in country furniture there (as well as in North America) was largely sparked by the growing awareness of the importance of social history. Simply put, country furniture was thought to be of insufficient importance to warrant serious study. Currently, much serious research in this area is being done, especially by members of the British Regional Furniture Society, an organization founded by Dr. Bernard D. Cotton in 1985 to promote the study and appreciation of regional furniture, particularly that which is called "country" furniture.[1] It was in collaboration with Dr. Cotton that the author curated the travelling exhibition, *Routes: Exploring the British Origins of Newfoundland Outport Furniture Design*, for the Newfoundland Museum, which opened at the Museum on Tuesday January 24, 1995.[2] Following this successful exhibit project, however, the focus of collecting and research in the material history curatorial area of the Museum, for which the author was responsible, had to shift from furniture to the fishery.[3] As a consequence, the important co-operative study of furniture design transmission from Britain to Newfoundland between the author and Dr. Cotton was virtually discontinued. Nevertheless, this challenging work has been kept alive, though only on a modest basis. For the most part, it has involved sending photographs of selected items of outport furniture to British colleagues for confirmation of their suspected British regional origin. In this regard, my Irish colleague, Mr. Matt McNulty, has been of invaluable assistance. But now that the author has taken early retirement from his position at the Newfoundland Museum, the funds required to continue this important work have simply been too difficult to acquire. Perhaps someone else eventually will pick up where the author has left off. In any case, it is hoped that, even without the contribution this material would have made, this book will succeed in giving at least some idea of the potential country furniture has for providing important cultural information and insights, as well as insights which have relevance far beyond regional geographic borders.

The author's Irish colleague, Matt McNulty, has enthusiastically remarked on several occasions: "Vernacular furniture is truly a testament to the ingenuity of humankind generally, and to the diversity of its expression". His wise words are especially relevant to outport furniture.

ENDNOTES

1. Members of the British Regional Furniture Society receive regular illustrated news-letters containing details of relevant exhibitions, book reviews, articles of general interest and events such as lectures, conferences, courses of study and workshops. Each spring the society also publishes a scholarly, well-illustrated journal, entitled *Regional Furniture*, which is sent to members only. Membership Secretary is Ms. Gerry Cotton, The Trouthouse, Warrens Cross, Lechlade, Glos. GL7 3DR, England.

2. *Routes: Exploring the British Origins of Newfoundland Outport Furniture Design* was a travelling exhibit produced by the Newfoundland Museum in St. John's. It was funded by a grant from the Museums Assistance Program, Department of Canadian Heritage, Government of Canada. As well, it received financial assistance from the Department of Tourism and Culture, Government of Newfoundland and Labrador. The exhibit represented the first critical examination of Canadian furniture jointly organized by British and Newfoundland furniture specialists. It consisted of forty-eight pieces of Newfoundland outport furniture, five pieces of English regional furniture and three items of Irish vernacular furniture. The Newfoundland pieces were displayed along with photographs and/or illustrations of their British counterparts. In addition to an introductory component, the three principal components were labelled "English Sources," "Irish Sources" and "Scottish and Other Sources." As well, there was a relatively small component that showed the type of hand tools used to make outport furniture and a component that displayed small Newfoundland items decorated with Celtic motifs. The exhibit was curated by Dr. Bernard D. Cotton and Walter Peddle.

3. At that time, the collapse of the Atlantic Canadian fishery became an ecological and social catastrophe for Newfoundland and Labrador, and consequently, one of the principal concerns of the Newfoundland Museum became the rapid disappearance of fishery-related items. Consequently, the Museum placed priority on collecting and researching such artifacts.

BIBLIOGRAPHY

Bird, Michael S. *Canadian Country Furniture*. Toronto: Stoddart 1994

Cook, Jane L. *Coalescence of Styles*. Montreal & Kingston London Ithaca: McGill-Queen's University Press 2001

Cotton, Bernard D. *The English Regional Chair*. 1990. Reprint, Woodbridge, Suffolk: Antique Collectors' Club 1991

Cotton, Bernard, and Walter Peddle. *Routes: Exploring the British Origins of Newfoundland Outport Furniture Design*. A Travelling Exhibition of the Newfoundland Museum. St. John's: Dunbar Studios 1995

Dobson, Henry, and Barbara Dobson. *The Early Furniture of Ontario and the Atlantic Provinces: A Record of the Pieces Assembled for the Country Heritage Loan Exhibition from Private Collections across Canada*. Toronto: M. F. Feheley 1974

Gilbert, Christopher. *English Vernacular Furniture (1750–1900)*. New Haven and London: Yale University Press 1991

Handcock, Gordon W. *So Long as There Comes No Women: Origins of English Settlement in Newfoundland*. St. John's: Breakwater 1989)

Kinmonth, Claudia. *Irish Country Furniture (1700–1950)*. New Haven, Conn.: Yale University Press 1993

Knell, David. *English Country Furniture: The National and Regional Vernacular, 1500–1900*. London: Barrie and Jenkins 1992

Loughnan, Nicholas. *Irish Country Furniture*. Irish Heritage Series, no. 46. Dublin: Eason and Son 1984

Lucie-Smith, Edward. *Furniture. A Concise History* London: Thames and Hudson Ltd. 1990

Mannion, John J. *Irish Settlements in Eastern Canada: A Study of Cultural Transfer and Adaptation*. Toronto: University of Toronto Press 1974

Pain, Howard. *The Heritage of Upper Canadian Furniture*. Toronto: Key Porter Books 1978

Peddle, Walter W. *The Forgotten Craftsmen*. St. John's: Harry Cuff Ltd. 1984

Peddle, Walter W. *The Traditional Furniture of Outport Newfoundland*. St. John's: Harry Cuff Ltd. 1983

LIST OF FIGURES

PHOTO CREDITS

All photographs are courtesy of the author except for those from the following whose co-operation the author gratefully acknowledges:

Provincial Museum of Newfoundland and Labrador (photos 2, 3, 8, 15, 39, 40, 62, 63, 151, 177, 229, 230, 235); Antonia McGrath (photos 55, 73, 84, 85, 90, 109, 110, 129, 130, 154, 155, 156, 169, 171, 185, 191, 204, 206, 217, 220, 224, 263, 288, 293, 294, 295, 302, 304, 305); Paterson Woodworking (photos 80 and 119); Gail Collins (photos 142, 143, 144, 145, 146, 147, 148); Hilary Cook (photos 158, 159, 163); *Toronto Daily Star* (photo 160); Royal Ontario Museum (photos 161 and 162); CMC (photo 219, Cultural Studies Division, 71-3197); and the late William Winter (photos 57 and 58).